"If we had a royal title of Queen of Promotion, the crown would belong to Carmen Leal. She probably knows more about promotion than anyone I've met in more than 25 years in the publishing business. Even more impressive, she doesn't just write and teach promotion, she goes out in the marketplace and does it."
—Cec Murphey, Award-winning author, co-author, and ghostwriter of more than eighty-eight books

"I had to make myself put *You Can Market Your Book* down to do other work. It is magnificent! Carmen's willingness to follow the "Master Builder" has resulted in her producing the master marketing resource for published authors. This is an indispensable tool for anyone who is published—or who hopes to be published."
—Sandy Brooks, Director, Christian Writers Fellowship International

"The dilemma of promoting Christian books is legendary: Publishers don't have the funds to adequately market their products, and authors are uncomfortable about calling attention to their good works. Well, help is at hand. Carmen Leal not only offers a step-by-step program that addresses HOW to promote worthy Christian books, but she also explains WHY it's essential that we do it. Her approach introduces the idea that writers and publishers are partners in producing life-changing reading material. If what we write can inspire people on their spiritual walk, we have an obligation to boost its visibility and availability."
—Holly G. Miller, Travel editor, Saturday Evening Post and Co-author of *Write on Target: A Five-Phase Program for Nonfiction Writers*

"Carmen Leal's latest book, *How to Market Your Book*, is invaluable to the author! This great book not only educates the author on innovative marketing strategies, but Carmen has intricately woven faith principles throughout the chapters that inspire and strengthen."
—Ken Wales, Executive Producer Film and Television, Author, *Sea of Glory— The Story of the Four Chaplains*

"I read *You Can Market Your Book* with a pen in hand, writing down tips and practical helps that made perfect sense to this author whose book was scheduled to be released within the month. I found so much valuable information in the first two chapters alone that I couldn't wait to finish the book!"
—T. Suzanne Eller, Author *Real Teens, Real Stories, Real Life*

"*You Can Market Your Book* is an excellent resource for authors, whether they are self-publishing their books or helping their publishing houses to promote them. Carmen Leal offers suggestions on seeking endorsements, choosing a title, and designing a press kit. She also gives ideas for marketing and developing a speaking platform. Tips from other professional writers add the icing on the cake."
—Susan Titus Osborn, Director of the Christian Communicator Manuscript Critique Service

"It's a hard reality that you as an author are the chief (sometimes only) marketer of your book. What you do can make the difference between 'Best Seller' and 'no seller.' In *You Can Market Your Book*, Carmen Leal not only shows why we must market but what to do and how to do it. With several chapters contributed by other specialists, the help Carmen gives in this book is essential to every serious author. It is a rich resource."
—Roger Palms, Author of *Effective Magazine Writing* and fourteen other books

"Carmen is a master teacher who has learned her lessons well and I'm thankful that she's willing to teach us how to market the books of our hearts. *You Can Market Your Book* needs to be added to the list of "must haves" for writers. It is the necessary element in completing the writing process."
—Jill Rigby, Author of *Manners of the Heart* and *Manners of the Heart At Home*

"*You Can Market Your Book* by Carmen Leal is an outstanding resource and one of the most comprehensive books I've seen on the topic. Authors who follow her practical, detailed, suggestions, are bound to be best-sellers!"
—LeAnn Thieman, co-author *Chicken Soup for the Christian Woman's Soul* and *Chicken Soup for the Nurse's Soul*

"Carmen Leal just created a near-perfect blueprint for publishing success with *You Can Market Your Book*. Treat yourself to this book the very day your manuscript is accepted for publication. Better yet, buy it as soon as you put pen to paper— after all, the builder studies a blueprint long before hammering the first nail."
—Wendy Lawton, Author of *Courage to Run, Tinker's Daughter* and *Almost Home*.

CARMEN LEAL

YOU CAN MARKET YOUR BOOK

ALL THE TOOLS YOU NEED TO SELL YOUR PUBLISHED BOOK

Write Now Publications
Phoenix, AZ 85013

You Can Market Your Book
Copyright ©2003 Carmen Leal
All rights reserved

Write Now Publications
Phoenix, Arizona

Cover Design by Eric Walljasper
Interior design by Pine Hill Graphics

Packaged by ACW Press
5501 N. 7th Ave., #502
Phoenix, Arizona 85013
www.acwpress.com
The views expressed or implied in this work do not necessarily reflect those of ACW Press. Ultimate design, content, and editorial accuracy of this work is the responsibility of the author(s).

Publisher's Cataloging-in-Publication
(Provided by Quality Books, Inc.)

Leal, Carmen, 1954-
    You can market your book : all the tools you need to
sell your published book / Carmen Leal.
    p. cm.
    ISBN 1-932124-00-4

    1. Books--Marketing. 2. Authors and publishers.
3. Publishers and publishing. I. Title.

Z283.L43 2003   002'.068'8
                          QBI03-200221

Printed in the United States of America.

To Gary. Finally.

Acknowledgments

Once again I send out my sincere thanks to three online writing groups. The wonderful friends on CWFI, CWG, and FCW have enriched my life and this book through their prayers, friendship, and in some cases, their ideas which are included in this book. Thanks go to a new group of ladies from the Advanced Writers and Speakers Association. Without you this book truly would not be as fun or helpful as I hope my readers find it once they delve inside and read your contributions.

Of course without my wonderful publisher, Steve Laube, there would be no book, so to him I give my thanks. My extraordinary editor, Lin Johnson, made me sound so much better than I ever thought possible and she isn't bothered by rush jobs. Thank you, Lin.

There are many experts who have helped me with each book and this one is no different. In various chapters the following people have shared their wisdom and have made this book more than I ever could have by myself. Special thanks got to Sheila Berndt, Steve and Lisa Carlson, Pamela Christian, Jim Cox, Kim Garrison, Judy Gann, Larry James, Ellie Kay, Kyle Liedtke, Marita Littauer, Deborah Raney, Amy Smith, Brian Taylor, John Vonhof, and Wendy Lawton.

And as always, I thank my Master Builder for trusting me with this book.

Contents

Foreword by Sally E. Stuart 11

Introduction: Beyond the Field of Dreams 13

Section One: *Project and Site Preparation*

1. The Blueprint: Marketing—Conception,
   Configuration, Creation 21
   What to Do and When to Do It: A Guide to Effective
   Book Publicity by Steve and Lisa Carlson. 28

2. Framing Your Project: The Title and Cover as a Sales Tool . . . 35

3. Insulate Your Structure: Endorsements,
   Reviews, Speaking Platforms. 45
   How the Book Review System Works by Jim Cox 57

Section Two: *Choosing the Right Tools and Materials*

4. Power Tools: Creating Winning
   Press Kits and Press Releases 65

5. Hand Tools: Promotions,
   Ad Specialties, Book Signings 79
   Cover Story by Deborah Raney 91
   Using Advertising Specialties to
   Sell Your Book by Sheila Berndt 94
   Twenty Ways to Make Your Book Signing
   an EVENT! by Larry James 97

6. Caulking the Gaps: Media Promotions 103
   12 Strategies for Your On-Camera Interview by Ellie Kay. 112
   Toto and the Wizard of Oz:
   Demystifying the Author Interview by Kyle Liedtke 117
   Writing an Interview Pitch that Gets
   You on the Air by Kim Garrison. 123

7. Climbing the Scaffold: Developing a Speaking Platform 131
   Speaking to Promote Your Book by Marita Littauer 138
   Speaker's Fees—Considering the Costs by Pamela Christian. . . 143

8. Finishing Touches: Online (Internet) Promotions 147
   Making an Ezine Work for
      Your Nonfiction Book by John Vonhof 169
   Web Design for Authors by Carmen Leal 171

Section Three: *Finding the Right Subcontractors*

9. Credentials and Credibility: Working with Professionals 183
   Book Design and Beyond by Brian Taylor. 197
   Putting the Airwaves to Work in
      Promoting Your Book by Amy Smith 208
   Marketing to Public Libraries by Judy Gann. 212

Section Four: *Executing Your Plan*

10. Open House: God-Inspired Author Success Stories 217
11. The Finished Product: Final Words 243

Recommended Books 249

Foreword
by Sally E. Stuart

When I started writing over 30 years ago and the term *marketing* was used, it was assumed you were referring to finding a publishing house for your book or other piece of writing. Back in those days—and even up to about ten years ago—you wrote a book; sold it to a house; and then moved on to the next project, confident the publisher would sell all those copies stacked neatly in the warehouse. And he usually did at least a fair job of that. How times have changed!

Today when we talk about marketing, it less often refers to finding the publisher—which it turns out could be the easier task—and more often refers to finding ways to get both the book and yourself as the author into the public eye. Almost weekly I get calls from newly published authors who are approaching a state of shock because they have just realized how much responsibility for the promotion of their books is going to fall on them.

Once that shock wears off and reality begins to set in, dedicated authors roll up their sleeves, ready to go to work. The question they ask me is: "Where do I begin?" It wasn't a question I could answer easily, so I can't tell you how happy I am that I can now recommend this volume—*You Can Market Your Book*.

Any time I'm looking for information in an area that is new to me, I first seek out those who know the answers because they have already been through the process and have learned the best path to follow. In the area of self-promotion, there is no one I know who is more knowledgeable on the subject—or better respected for what she has accomplished in the promotion of her own books—than Carmen Leal. I'm thankful that she's willing to share what she has learned with the rest of us who are often both new to this process—and terrified at the prospect of promoting ourselves.

Most of us are uncomfortable with and unaccustomed to tooting our own horns, so the whole process of self-promotion is foreign to our nature. That was one of the first personal battles I had to fight as a young author. In the midst of that battle, one of my early mentors said something to the effect that if we didn't believe enough in what we had written—in the message God had given us—to actually share it with the world, how could we expect anyone else to do it for us? When I reached the point where I fully understood the importance of her words, I was ready to take on the task of self-promotion. I only wish there had been a resource like this one to guide me along that not yet clearly defined pathway. It's comforting to know that this book will help make that path less obscure.

Although you may be starting with overwhelming feelings of self-doubt, rest assured that when you complete your journey through these pages, you will not only know where to start, but also which steps will move you toward success. God has given you a unique message to share through the book or books you have written, so what better way to honor the trust God has put in you than to get that message out to a waiting world. As you climb that ladder of success, keep in mind that your place is on the rung behind the Lord—not the one ahead of Him.

You Can Market Your Book is a good how-to title that delivers what it promises. But if each time you read it you repeat it as *You Can Market Your Book,* it will also be a personal promise that we can fulfill the task before us. This is a book you will want to read for overall knowledge on the subject, but also one you will come back to again and again as you plot your promotional journey.

Beyond the Field of Dreams

"If you build it, he will come."

—W. P. Kinsella, Shoeless Joe

In the 1989 movie *Field of Dreams*, based on the book *Shoeless Joe* by W. P. Kinsella, an Iowa farmer named Ray hears a mysterious voice in his corn field. He interprets the message, "If you build it, he will come," as a call to build a baseball field on his farm. He eventually builds the field, and the ghosts of Shoeless Joe Jackson and the other seven Chicago White Sox players banned from the game for throwing the 1919 World Series appear and play.

This plot made for one of the greatest baseball movies ever; and even I, who think America's pastime should be changed to basketball, enjoyed it immensely. When the team congregated to play on Ray's field of dreams, it was truly magical. He built it and they came.

I teach at a number of writers' conferences each year and love sharing my knowledge with writers. I especially enjoy hearing a new writer's vision for her book at individual appointments. My mother told me I was a pragmatic child; and this trait has proven valuable as I hear yet another author say, "God told me to write this."

I never doubt a writer's passion for his project. Passion is a must for digging in and making the commitment needed to produce a book. I also never doubt that God told someone to take the circumstances of her life and weave them into a format for others to read. I wrote my first book, *Faces of Huntington's* (Essence), because of that passion and the knowledge that God had called me to write a book for the thousands of families suffering from such a devastating disease.

I do have a problem with the inevitable, yet passionate writer who says, "If I write it I know it will sell because God told me to write it." My response rarely varies. "Ah, but did God tell an editor to publish it? Did God tell your future audience to buy it?"

I try to ask these questions in a gentle way, followed by a discussion on the various forms of publication to discover if that passion is really a book or maybe an article. Hopefully, by the time our conversation is over, the writer has several options to consider and our discussion, coupled with what he or she has learned at a writers' conference, was time well spent.

Every publisher must be a good steward of his company's resources. Like any other business, there are salaries, overhead, royalties, and other expenses. Every effort must be made to make a profit on each book published. Without profitability the publisher is not being a good steward and will most likely cease to exist.

I knew God wanted me to write *Faces of Huntington's,* but that pragmatism, and ten years as a marketing consultant, helped me understand that my book was better suited to self-publishing. According to newly revised figures from the Huntington's Disease Society of America, approximately 40,000 persons have Huntington's Disease in the United States. Because this is a genetic disease, the number of individual families affected is substantially fewer.

The book falls into a niche, or specific, category; only a narrow percentage of the population is interested in the topic. Because of my direct knowledge of Huntington's Disease and how to reach those potential readers, my book was perfect for niche marketing. As a result of listening to God, writing a good book, getting professional editing and production, and being willing to work very hard, *Faces of Huntington's* has done well. More importantly, it has helped thousands of families.

My third book, *WriterSpeaker.com,* was published by Shaw/Water-Brook, a division of Random House. Because it had a potentially larger market, and because the publisher already had a history of publishing books for writers, I never considered self-publishing. I worked just as hard to generate a buzz and sell books released through a royalty publisher as I did with my self-published title.

The other day a member of one of my e-mail discussion lists told me she is writing a book about her passion. She said, "If I write it, and it is well written, I know it will sell." I've heard variations on her statement more often than I can count; but somehow, seeing it one more time made me realize the need for a book for Christians about marketing their published books.

The good news is that it's easy to publish a book because of self-publishing, print-on-demand, electronic publishing, and desktop publishing. The bad news is that most people fail to understand that it's not a matter of, "If you write it, they will buy it."

You Can Market Your Book is designed to help you understand basic book marketing principles. Yes, your book might have been published by a larger, traditional publisher; but unless you are a superstar author, you are the main salesperson. You might have distribution and you might even have a publicist for a brief time, but even with the "big boys" it is ultimately up to you. You need to be as aggressive as possible if you want to reclaim your garage or closets from the boxes of unsold books or if you expect a royalty check from your publisher.

This book is filled with practical, low-cost ideas, strategies, and case studies designed to get your book to the people who need it. In the November 2000 issue of *Publishing Success* I wrote, "Make sure that you understand the 80/20 rule: Writing takes only 20 percent of your effort, marketing and promotion takes up the other 80 percent" (p. 40). Three years later I believe it more than ever. Marketing may not come naturally to you, but there are hundreds of ways to get your book into the hands of your readers. I might not believe, "If you write it, they will buy it"; but I do believe if you write a good book and market it well, they will buy it.

How to Use This Book

When the publisher and I first discussed this book, we talked about it as a resource for self-published authors. As I started talking to authors at conferences and online, royalty published authors shared how ill equipped they felt to market their own books and how most publishers expect authors to help in this area.

There are already many excellent book marketing resources available; so I decided if I was going to write a book, it would have to meet the needs of all published authors. This is not a book on how to self-publish your book. This book assumes you or your publisher has already learned about the publishing industry. Several books listed in the appendix should guide you in the right direction if you'd like to learn more.

Marketing tips and strategies are sprinkled throughout each chapter; so even if you already know a great deal about a topic, you might want to quickly scan that section and see what new ideas are included. I've also asked over a dozen recognized professionals to share their knowledge in articles at the end of several chapters.

The companion Web site at www.writerspeaker.com/youcan.html features every Web link in the book as well as several worksheets and forms. As you go through this book, you'll find references to a ten-point Web site evaluation form, a promotional calendar, and other documents. Once you get to the above site you'll be able to download and print these materials.

The detailed table of contents and appendix should help you in each step of your marketing journey. I pray God's blessing on your books, and it is my sincere wish that *You Can Market Your Book* helps you take God's message to the world.

Section One

Project Planning

Chapter

The Blueprint
Marketing—Conception, Configuration, Creation

Cherish your visions and your dreams as they are

the children of your soul, the blueprints of your

ultimate achievements.

—Napoleon Hill

I n 1963 Sidney Poitier won an Oscar for his portrayal of a young man who reluctantly gets involved with a group of German-speaking nuns living in the Arizona desert. In *Lilies of the Field*, Mother Superior persuades Homer Smith, an unemployed handyman, to build them a chapel, or, as she says, a "shapel." She is convinced that "Schmitt" has been sent from above to help her realize her dream. He protests loudly, but she will not be dissuaded. Eventually, the project becomes equally important to Homer; and through this delightful film, we learn to never underestimate the divine tools that we are given and the importance of sharing our gifts.

Homer never wanted to build a "shapel" for a group of nuns in the middle of nowhere, and I never wanted to write a book. Maybe you never wanted to be a writer; but after circumstances taught you more than you ever wanted to know, you felt the need to share what you learned with others. Even if you did want to be a writer, taking that first step was probably a challenge.

With trepidation you started writing, checked out every grammar book in the library; joined a critique group; went to conferences; continued to write; and somehow, through the traditional route or the self-published one, you have a book. You managed to scale the "Alps" of a learning curve and found out it could be done. After the initial exhilaration of holding your new book in your hands, you begin to panic. In front of you is the "Mt. Everest" of learning curves. Ahead of you is marketing. Now what?

Lisa Crayton, editor of *Spirit-Led Writer,* a magazine for Christian writers, says, "Our attitudes will determine our altitudes, the level of our success. If we see failure or nonopportunity, we will be less motivated to work. If we keep our eyes on Jesus Christ and see by the eyes of faith, we will achieve success—eventually."

Once Homer in *Lilies of the Field* knew he had no choice but to build the chapel, he drew a plan, or a blueprint. In his case it was a simple drawing, but it kept him on course. When his helpers added beams or placed windows or doors in the wrong place, he was able to show them his drawing and redirect them to his original vision. Homer's plan was basic, as was the chapel. Building a cathedral in the desert would have been overkill, so an intricate blueprint wasn't needed.

Any author with a published or soon-to be-released book needs a blueprint, or marketing plan. Your plan might be basic or intricate, depending on your book and your goals. For example, if your book is about the history of a small town and targeted to its residents, your plan might be relatively small. If, however, you have written a mystery with a potentially large audience, your plan will be grander in scale. Of course, your budget will also play a part in how you market your book.

Either way, your plan means choosing the right approach, contacting the right people, and understanding that doing it right takes time. We're back to that 80/20 rule.

What is a Marketing Plan?

In *Lillies of the Field* Mother Superior saw Homer Smith as someone who could build her "shapel." Their adversarial relationship escalated until Homer declared,"I ain't no nun. I'm nobody you can boss around. I ain't building no chapel. I ain't no contractor."

Not one to be daunted, Mother Superior cried, "Alright we build it. We women. We will. It's God's will."

I'm sure Homer was surprised to hear himself saying, "I'll clean the site so the women won't break their backs hauling off beams." After he said it he had no choice but to clear the foundation.

A marketing plan is the foundation of how you will reach your targeted audience. It can be exhaustive or basic, depending on your budget, interest, willingness to work, and level of success that is important to you.

As Christians, the first step in our marketing plan must be prayer. It doesn't stop with your readers though. Every step of the writing and marketing process should be bathed in prayer. Though you may feel alone in your marketing maze, you're not. Printers, design and advertising specialty professionals, media hosts, bulk mailing companies, and others will become part of your marketing team. Begin praying that God will direct you to the right, ethical people who will catch your enthusiasm and work with you to promote your book.

The second step in your preparation is to produce something of excellence. Of course, books need to be excellent in content; but the design, packaging, and marketing efforts also need to be polished. Seems overwhelming, doesn't it?

John Vonhof, author of a self-published book, *Fixing Your Feet: Prevention and Treatment for Athletes* (Footwork), believes in personalized excellence as a way of serving his readers. His book is for athletes who use their feet as their primary mode of transportation. "They do things to their feet that the average person does not do and, as a result, have problems galore. *Fixing Your Feet* gives them a host of ideas for prevention and treatments."

John knows that everyone's feet are unique, and there are different ways of fixing problems for each person. "I give them hope by informing them of what their options are, the products and where to find them. I also share stories of what others have done in each major area of foot care. Other books that cover foot care are more general in nature and do not offer the depth as mine."

John's commitment to excellence is paying off. "Sales are higher in the past six months then ever before. I suspect a third edition by spring 2003. It has become the 'bible' of foot care for athletes, and I have just touched the surface of the potential market."

Like my Huntington's books and other niche market books, John's book isn't a runaway best-seller; but through knowing and serving his reader, he has impressive market penetration.

Even if your book is not destined to hit *The New York Times* best-seller list, you can still think big. Our books can reach the world for Christ. What is bigger than that?

Plan Preparation

If you remember nothing else about that high school journalism class, you probably remember these six questions: Who? What? Where? When? How? and Why? The answers to these questions constitute the bulk of your preparation.

Who?

You identified who you wrote your book for before and as you were writing, so this should be easy. Who do you wish to serve through your words? In marketing terms, who is your primary target market? Who is your core market? How large is your audience?

The more tightly you can focus your answers to these questions, the more effective your marketing efforts will be. Women as a target audience is too broad. How many different markets are there for women? Some write t books for mothers of small children, while others focus on single women or those facing loss. Do you see how saying women represent a core market is too broad?

You'll notice I used the word *primary*. I think of my primary market as being who I most desire to reach with a book. They become the basis for my potential profit. Making a profit is not the number one reason most of us write; but without an income from our books, we can't afford to keep writing. Many of you chose an alternative publishing route, and that means you invested some money in the project. Reaching your primary market means you will have an income stream to reimburse yourself and, hopefully, be able to write more books.

Defining your audience often is easier with a nonfiction book than with a novel, but it needs to be done no matter what you write. Most books have a primary target market, followed by additional potential markets. With *Faces of Huntington's*, my primary reader was, and continues to be, families who are currently dealing with the disease. They might have it themselves, or they could be caregivers or be at risk. Maybe their children or other loved ones have died from it. These are people who are hungry for information about Huntington's Disease. Other people who might have an interest would be members of the medical profession; pastors or chaplains; hospice workers; friends of the affected family; and even people dealing with a related disorder, such as Parkinson's, Alzheimer's, and multiple sclerosis. How I make sure these people hear about my book differs with each group.

My target market is specific, so the key is to find ways to reach them. My goal—and it's an unrealistic goal—is to reach everyone in my primary market or, in marketing terms, have 100 percent market penetration. I know this will never happen for several reasons. One reason is that not everyone reads to get information. As writers, we expect that the entire population reads as voraciously as we do, but it just isn't so. Another reason I know I will never reach every person affected by Huntington's is that it is an international disease. While a large portion of my market lives in an English-speaking country, there are tens of thousands who don't.

With my primary market and, to a degree, my secondary ones, I know where they live and how to reach them through national associations, real-life and Internet groups, etc. This is true to a lesser degree with others who might gain from reading my book, but there are still specific ways to connect with those markets.

WriterSpeaker.com has a huge potential market, but that doesn't mean I'll necessarily sell more books or sell them any easier. Everyone is a writer these days. When I offer a course at my local library or through continuing education I am amazed at the turnout. I recently did a two-hour workshop on the topic of writing a nonfiction book. There were over seventy-five budding authors willing to give up a Saturday morning to learn how to fulfill their dream.

My primary market for *You Can Market Your Book* is anyone who already is or wants to be a published book author. That's a significant number of people, but it's often difficult to find them. Then there are the other markets, such as family members of these writers who want to give the book as a gift or publishers who might buy copies for their authors.

What?

Lots of questions fall into this category. What is the essence of your book? The inherent value of each book needs to be stated in one sentence. My one sentence for this book is: "Practical, lowcost ideas and case studies guaranteed to get your book to the people who need it."

What is your competition? Stop right there. You do have competition. I can count over a dozen well-written books that are similar to mine. I can only think of one or two that have somewhat of a Christian focus, but those books differ in other areas. Most of the totally secular books don't have worksheets to guide the writer, and some don't have case studies that provide a show-and-tell element. Knowing my competition not only helps me write a stronger book to fit the needs of my audience, but it strengthens my marketing plan.

What makes my book unique? What do the publishers of competitive titles do to promote their titles? What is my marketing budget?

Do you see how asking questions can help you create a more defined marketing plan?

Where?

Where will you find your customers? The first answer that pops into your head might be bookstores. Unless you write mainstream fiction for an established publisher, have a book on Oprah's book club, or are a best-selling author, the bookstore is almost the last place to find your customer.

If your book isn't represented by a distributor—and most small press books aren't—getting on a bookshelf is almost impossible. Even having distribution doesn't guarantee success. The books that make it onto bookshelves are the ones that either go by default or those that a sales rep recommends to the bookstore owner or buyer. With an overwhelming number of books in print and a massive number represented by the distributor, the sales rep isn't going to know about your book, much less recommend it.

So where will you find your readers? This is an important question to answer as you are creating your marketing plan, and it differs depending on the type of book you have written. If you write for children, you might do school visits or sell to libraries. Writing for those who have gone through a divorce means you'll need to contact national and regional divorce support groups and offer your book as a resource for their clients. John Vonhof, author of *Fixing Your Feet: Prevention and Treatments for Athletes*, goes for the obvious and finds his customers at marathons, sporting goods and shoes stores, foot doctors, and a host of other nonbookstore locations.

When?

When should you start marketing your book? Now! Even if you're reading this in anticipation of writing a book or if you're almost finished with you manuscript, the time to market is now. Marketing starts with knowing your reader and his or her needs, and that's part of the writing process. A marketing calendar written by Steve and Lisa Carlson can be found after this chapter. It should help you better understand when to ask for reviews, send out galleys and direct mail, create your Web site, schedule book signings, and more.

Why?

Why do you have to worry about marketing plans? The answer is simple: because you want to get your books into the hands of those who need it. Most books published through traditional publishers have an initial print run of 5,000 copies or less. Books go out of print much more quickly than any author would like to think is possible; but when you consider that fewer than half of all books published go into a second printing, you can see why it's critical that you be a marketing guru for your book.

No one knows your book better or cares more passionately than you. If you still have trouble understanding why you need to eat, sleep, and breathe marketing, then go back to the last sentence of the introduction of this book. I might not believe the slogan "If you write it, they will buy it"; but I do believe if you write a good book and market it well, they will buy it.

How?

How will you reach your reader? This is the fun part of your marketing plan. In future chapters I'll discuss getting reviews, building and marketing Web sites, doing book signings, speaking as a marketing tool, and lots of other tips and strategies.

"What to Do and When to Do It: A Guide to Effective Book Publicity" by Steve and Lisa Carlson is featured at the end of this chapter. This article includes a promotional calendar that should help you create your marketing plan and budget.

Featured Authors

Lisa Crayton   www.spiritledwriter.com
John Vonhof   www.footworkpub.com
Steve and Lisa Carlson   www.upperaccess.com

What to Do and When to Do It
A Guide to Effective Book Publicity

by Steve and Lisa Carlson

Following is a general outline of the basic steps to take in promoting a title. A few of the steps are identified as optional, and
a few are obviously appropriate only for nonfiction. The most
brilliant publicity campaigns, of course, also contain original,
one-of-a-kind elements. With those caveats, this document
should provide a good start in developing publicity plans.

The timing revolves around the official **publication date.** This
is the arbitrary date that you will list in your submission to
Bowker for *Books in Print.* It is usually some time after books are
expected to be printed and in stock.

Before committing yourself to publishing . . .

- Determine, as objectively as possible, the potential audience
  for the book. If it's nonfiction, who will benefit from the
  information? What other books have similar information,
  and why is this one better?
- Make notes on how to reach the intended audience. Are
  there organizations that will help spread the word? Are there
  specific publications that target your audience? Is the book
  likely to be carried by libraries? The answers to those questions will not only help determine how marketable the book
  will be, but may also influence the final writing, editing, and
  design of the book. As random examples, you may want to

Steve and Lisa Carlson have been in the publishing industry for twenty years.
Their company, Upper Access, publishes books and provides publicity services
and business software for other publishers. Visit their Web site at www.upper-
access.com or call 802-482-2988 to learn more. Copyright © 2002 by Upper
Access, Inc. Permission is granted to reproduce this document as long as it is
reproduced in full, including this copyright statement and contact information
for Upper Access, Inc. Partial reproduction or other use is prohibited unless
permission is specifically granted by Upper Access, Inc.

credit an expert who can help you, and add an index to make the book more attractive to librarians.

Eight months before publication date . . .

- Submit the title to the Library of Congress for PCN and, if appropriate, CIP data. Also submit to Bowker for *Forthcoming Books in Print*. (Bowker submission may be revised on-line later for changes in number of pages, etc.) Initiate detailed planning of the promotional campaign.

Six months before publication date . . .

- At this time, major editing should be completed. If you are combining elements of typesetting with the editing process, the format of the book should be taking shape. It should be very readable, even though finishing touches are still needed.
- Ideally, you should prepare a "pre-galley," trimmed and bound in book form. If the typesetting is not far enough along for that, make neat manuscript copies, comb-bound or otherwise convenient to read. Send these with requests for cover blurbs or other endorsements. Also send them to editors of publications with whom you wish to discuss serial rights or other publication rights.

Four months before publication date . . .

- Bound galleys must be prepared and shipped to the major reviewers who need them. This means that editing and type-setting are in nearly final form so that the pages can be duplicated and bound. The cover art should also be in nearly final form so that color printouts or photos (of at least the front cover) can be included with the galleys. Generally, between twelve and twenty galleys will be sent with pitch letters.
- Galleys should also be sent to others who need advance information, including any trade distributor (if you have one) and major wholesalers.
- Final proofreading, typesetting, and cover design should be completed as soon as possible, so that files may be created and sent to the printer.

- Brochures or fliers should be prepared for any early publicity, but in relatively small numbers, because new materials will be needed when the reviews and other quotable comments start coming in.

Three months before publication date . . .

- This is a good time to follow up on the bound galleys that were sent to major reviewers. Usually the best approach is by telephone, but check their guidelines on the Web to be sure.
- If you have an active Web site, the book should be listed and strongly promoted by now, with provisions in place for taking advance orders. You may want to also adopt a separate Web site just for the book. If you work with a fulfillment company such as Book Clearing House, make sure all the materials are provided for its site. You may want to consider a site with BookZone, with a listing in its Super Catalog.

Two months before publication date . . .

- Finished books are likely to arrive from the printer at about this time. Ideally, you should already have media lists, press releases, and press kits ready to go, with or without review copies.
- Mail the first round of review copies. Numbers will vary (from as few as twenty to as many as a thousand, sometimes more) depending on a great many considerations. A very carefully selected mail list is essential.
- The nature of the press kit accompanying the review copies will also vary greatly. Depending on the situation, it may be just a press release and pitch letter enclosed with the book. In other cases it is worthwhile to create an attractive folder with many additional materials.
- News releases should also be sent to many other media—usually at least 2,000. The preferred method for this is usually fax, but in some instances e-mail may also be acceptable. Regular mail has advantages, because one can enclose sidebars and other material, but has been in disfavor recently because of Anthrax scares. In most cases, a review copy should be offered if the person receiving this material requests it.

- Participation in the BookSense Advance program should be considered.
- The book should be listed by Amazon, Barnes and Noble, and other major Web stores. If the listings are minimal, supply the material needed for enhancements.

One month before publication date . . .

- Be sure to send finished books to every major reviewer who received a bound galley, even if there is no review. Sometimes, this can make a last-minute difference, particularly if it's a very attractive book. At the very least, this is a courtesy to major reviewers whom you will be approaching again when you release another book.
- By now you should know whether you are receiving reviews from the advance galleys you sent to library publications such as *Library Journal* and *Booklist*. If there are favorable reviews in these publications, start making arrangements to print fliers quoting the reviews to be mailed in library mailing programs. Small advertisements in library publications quoting the reviews may also be worthwhile.
- This is a good time to start making arrangements for book signings and talks at stores and other venues such as libraries.

On the publication date . . .

- As of this date, you can no longer use words such as "advance" and "forthcoming" in promoting the book, but you can still call it "new" for a few weeks or even months. This is a good day to tie up loose ends. Are there important magazines that haven't yet received review copies? Does it seem appropriate to fax a second press release to a new list? Did you remember to send a press release to your Alma Mater to include in its alumni publications? How about your local weekly? Have you brought a book to the manager of your local bookstore and asked if a signing can be arranged? Have you followed up with contacts who have already received materials?
- This is also a good time to take a new look at your publicity program, to see if any mid-course changes are in order. How

you proceed from here depends in part on how your publicity has been received so far. (If everything has been disappointing so far, don't give up! We all want instant success, but, historically, some of the biggest-selling books have failed to become popular until years after publication.)

• Publication day is also a good time to break out the champagne with your spouse/partner and anybody else who has been helpful and supportive. Don't forget to send thank-you notes and free copies to people who gave you cover quotes, provided information, or performed other good deeds to help make possible this great book.

After the publication date . . .

• If your author is an articulate speaker, start a campaign of broadcast appearances, which can continue as long as the book remains in print.

• Bookstore signings and library readings can also continue long after the book is in print.

• When people tell you they like the book, encourage them to write a review for Amazon and BN.com.

• Monitor the media. If a news event occurs that overlaps with the book's subject matter, contact journalists covering the events and fax news releases with your author's comments. If the subject is back in the news frequently, consider faxes with new angles once a month or more.

• Consider listing your author in the various reference books and on Web sites of experts available for interview by journalists.

• Consider subscribing to a service such as ProfNet, which connects journalists with experts (your authors). If you have only one or two authors who are likely to benefit, then it will probably be less expensive to work with a PR company that subscribes to the service.

• If you did not receive early reviews from major library publications, work hard to get write-ups in other publications that are respected by librarians. Some of them will review books after the publication date. With appropriate reviews you'll be able to sell thousands of books to libraries. Without the reviews you'll sell almost none.

- If a book has suffered from inadequate early promotion, it is possible to undertake a media blitz for an older title. If a book has done well early on but sales have declined sharply, create new promotions to revive public interest. It's never too late to launch a new publicity campaign for a book that is well written and well produced, with information that is still valid.

Featured Resources

Book Clearing House	www.book-clearing-house.com
BookSense	www.BookSense.com
Books in Print	www.bookwire.com
Library of Congress (Copyright)	www.loc.gov/copyright

Chapter

Framing Your Project
The Title and Cover As a Sales Tool

If you prepare yourself at every point as well as you can, with whatever means you have…you will be able to grasp opportunity for broader experience when it appears. Without preparation, you cannot do it.

— Eleanor Roosevelt

L et's get back to the part of the movie *Lilies of the Field* where Homer eventually decides to build the "chapel." After he tells Mother Maria he'll help, he explains, "Can't do work without good tools." He then outlines the three things needed for good results: a plan, the right materials, and good labor.

Your book's title and cover are two important building materials. In fact, they, along with the content, are the cornerstones of your marketing plan. There are lots of marketing ideas and strategies in this book; but unless you have the right title, cover, and content, selling your book will be more difficult, if not impossible.

Choosing the right title and subtitle is critical for your book's success. Some of your books already have a title, or you won't have a say in what your book is called. It's still worth understanding the importance of a title for future projects.

I know that before I can write an outline or plot a book, I need a good working title. The title might change, but having something from the beginning brings my book to life. Most novels don't have a subtitle, so the perfect title is even more critical.

Of course, a great title has to deliver; and if the content is not something readers want or is poorly executed, the book will not sell. But a bad title will hide a good book from potential customers.

I interviewed authors about the importance of titles, and everyone who responded agreed that titles need to be a reflection of the author's mission. Janet Holm McHenry, author of *Prayerwalk* and *Daily Prayerwalk* (WaterBrook), captured everyone's comments when she said, "The title is critical. It needs to strike right at the reader's felt need. People don't buy a book unless they think it'll meet a clear felt need."

Author, speaker, and popular radio broadcaster Virelle Kidder says, "My perspective is that titles should grab the reader's attention and either point clearly to a felt need that the book deals with or evoke a feeling that, along with the cover design, hits a felt need. Sometimes this is impossible, but it influenced me a lot in choosing books for radio interviews."

Her books, *Mothering Upstream; Loving, Launching, and Letting Go;* and *Getting the Best Out of Public Schools* (Broadman & Holman), co-authored with her husband, Dr. Steven Kidder, both point to felt needs. The second title is so tightly written that a subtitle isn't needed.

Brenda Nixon has defined her audience and her particular niche by calling her book *Parenting Power in the Early Years: Raising Your Child with Confidence, Birth to Age Five*. With one glance it's obvious this is a parenting book for parents who want to have power that only knowledge can bring. The subtitle tells us that Brenda wishes to serve parents of children from birth to five years old.

Sometimes you think you know exactly who your niche audience is for a certain book, and you're pleasantly surprised to see your audience expanded beyond that circle. For example, Kari West and Noelle Quinn wrote a divorce-specific book, *When He Leaves: Choosing to Live, Love, and Laugh Again* (Cook). "Never in my wildest imagination did I ever think that one of that book's audiences would be women experiencing broken engagements," says Kari. "However, in the four years since its release, I've received numerous letters from young women in their 20s whose fiancés took a hike only days before the wedding; and they were devastated. 'By the time I finished the last chapter, I was smiling,' one reader said. 'I realize my fiancé is the loser, not me.'"

A great fiction title is equally important and should also be tied into the readers' need. That need might be more subtle, but it is still there. The genre in which you are writing plays a big part in knowing how to title your book. Escapism, romance, adventure, mystery, and travel are just a few of the needs readers want met when they pick up a novel. Your title and the cover, of course, must immediately tell them your book will not only meet that need but will entertain them along the way.

"My first title," explains Eva Marie Everson, "Was *Shadow Fall,* so named because the main character is "falling through a shadow." My co-author and I wove in several metaphors about shadows, darkness and light. The editors liked the shadowy part, but *Shadow Fall* had since been taken."

Her co-author, Francis Chadwick, threw out a number of humorous suggestions. In the middle of the flurry of e-mails, he referenced *Hamlet,* Act 2, Scene II, "the very substance of the ambitious is merely the shadow of a dream."

"I just fell in love with *Shadow of Dreams,* not only because of the meaning behind the line, but because there are a few dream scenes. It was perfect. I felt—as did the editors—that it had just the right edge for a suspense novel's title."

Eva Marie's readers have a need for edge-of-the-seat novels, and her title gave promise that they would not be disappointed.

How do you find the right title?

Eva Marie found the title to the *Shadow of Dreams* (Barbour) sequel while listening to a song by Loreena McKennitt called "Mummer's Dance." When she heard the line about shadows, she knew she had found her title: *Summon the Shadows.*

Kari West explains how she finds her titles. "I go deep into my own heart and try to pull out frustrations and/or longings I've experienced, then craft a book title, chapter title, and subtitles accordingly that express what the reader is feeling." In other words, she is identifying a need and then writing a book to meet that need.

"My second book, *Dare to Trust, Dare to Hope Again: Living With Losses of the Heart* (Cook), could have been a horror story because I violated my own rule," Kari relates. "I chose *In God's Arms of Mercy* as the title. Now I realize that title is quite nebulous and does not express what the book is really about. This book was released September 10, 2001, one day before the catastrophic loss of life at the Trade Center in New York City. Neither [my editor] Julie nor I had a clue just how appropriate 'daring to trust and hope' would be for so many who are grieving and for those of us who remain anxious about the future.'"

A strong theme can lead you to a title that could be a key to selling your book to an editor or agent. Linda Fulkerson is self-publishing her book *The Prodigal Daughter: Hope for Runaway Christians and Those Who Await Their Return*, but she also managed to snag the attention of an agent with her compelling title and subtitle. Linda explains, "He said the title 'grabbed' him. However, he continued to say that none of the chapter titles or the supporting material I sent supported the title and the expectations it gave to the would-be reader."

This was valuable information that few editors or agents typically pass on to unpublished writers. Because Linda had hooked him with her title, he was willing to work with her on suggestions and revisions.

Once a book is published, the wrong title can adversely affect book sales and play a huge role in keeping your book out of the hands of those readers who need your words to meet their needs. Sharon Jaynes knows firsthand what a difference titles can make to the success of a project. "My first book had a great title. However, my publisher didn't like it and changed it to *At Home With God: Stories of Life, Love and Laughter*. I begged them not to use that title. My agent begged right along with me. We even gave them several other clever options to pick from. However, they would not budge."

"I felt the title didn't tell what the book was about. To me it sounded like someone had died and gone to Heaven—not that that would be a bad thing—but just not what the book was about. Their argument was that the subtitle would clear that up."

Sharon had many opportunities to see people's responses to the title. "Every time that book was on a book table with my other books, people would have questions. They knew exactly what *Being a Great Mom, Raising Great Kids* was about. They knew exactly what *Celebrating a Christ-Centered Christmas* was about. They knew what *Seven Life Principles for Every Woman* was about. But then they would get to *At Home*, look puzzled, and ask, 'What's this one about?' If they posed that question to me, I could only imagine their response in a lonely aisle in a bookstore."

She goes on to explain the fate of that book. "All three of my other books have done very well. *At Home* is going out of print. I will be getting my rights back and publishing it with another publisher—with a different title, I might add!"

Your book will be listed in Bowker's *Books in Print* by title, author, and subject. If you add a keyword in the title that is the same as the subject, you will double your exposure. *Books in Print* is only one database where your book will be listed, and the more concise you are the better chance you have to be found.

Choosing the Title

People choose titles in a variety of ways. A phrase from your book, a character's name, or even the book's topic can help you find that elusive word or words. Even newspaper headlines, song and movie lines or titles, and snippets of conversation are all places to begin looking for a title.

Once you have a topic for your book and you know who your market is, pull together some possible titles. A short, intuitive, descriptive title with a more lengthy, explanatory subtitle makes it obvious where to shelve your book or how to position it in a catalog. A concise, easily remembered title can be used as a domain name that can be quickly found by search engines.

A visit to an online bookstore, such as Amazon.com, or your local bookstore or library is an excellent way to find out not only what else has been written on your subject, but what titles have been used. Titles are not protected under copyright laws, so it is possible to accidentally title your book the same as something already in print. Looking at books can spur the creative juices and lead you to the right title.

Playing off the title of a popular movie is how author Caron Loveless found the title of her next book, *Honey, They Shrunk My Hormones* (Howard). Or playing off of another best-seller, Mike Nappa wrote *Who Moved My Church?* (RiverOak).

Prayer is also important in choosing your title, as it is with every area of our lives. Sometimes it's only after a book's release that we can see how God guided an author to choose the perfect title.

Your future readers can also help choose your book title. Polls and contests are fun ways to involve others in the selection. Web sites are excellent places to get feedback and even to post a daily tally that will drive traffic to your site. You might find the perfect title and get visitors to your site while adding excitement to the process.

The right title compels readers to explore the back cover for clues that will convince them this book will meet specific needs. It must be easy to say and easy to remember. For help on writing such a title that will be a solid marketing tool, use the worksheet on my Web site, www.writerspeaker.com/youcan.html.

The Cover

The cover of the book is not only a nifty way to keep pages clean and in order. That's certainly one purpose; but if it was the only one, all books would come in brown paper wrapping. A cover's primary function is to act as a fantastic sales tool.

If a royalty house is publishing your book, you might not have much say in your cover design. Many of you self-published your book; and whether it's printed and bound or an electronic book, you should have given as much attention to the cover as any major publisher. Some alternative publishing companies offer cover design as part of their package. Before signing a contract, ask to see several finished books to review not only their quality, but their cover concepts and execution. Make sure to ask if the cover came to the publisher camera ready from the author or if the publisher's artist did the work.

Depending on who you quote, estimates vary from one to five minutes about how long the average consumer looks at your book before deciding to buy. (My publisher, Steve Laube, who worked in the bookstore business for over a decade, claims it is usually no more than thirty seconds.) With 1.5 million books in print, or even 135,000 new titles published in the United States in 2001, you can imagine the competition.

Your cover will make an impression on the buyer as will the spine and the back cover. It will make an impression on retail customers, trade show visitors, and bookstore and catalog buyers. The question is: What kind of impression will it make?

The intent of this book is not to teach you everything you ever wanted to know about graphics and typography. There are many professionals who can help you with your book cover. There are also wonderful books to serve as references. The purpose in discussing covers is not to teach you how to design the perfect cover, but to emphasize the importance of the cover as a sales tool. Unless you have a strong graphics and marketing background in the area of publishing, or at least in packaging, I recommend using a professional designer for this all-important step in creating your book. Brian Taylor, of Pneuma Design, is one such professional. His must-read discussion of various book-design components is invaluable and appears in chapter nine.

Here are a few points to consider when creating your own cover or working with a professional designer:

- The most important information should be at the top. Unless you are a best-selling author, this usually means your title.
- The cover should match the contents of the book.
- Follow genre-specific formats when creating your cover.
- Simple and uncluttered is a good rule to follow.
- Easy-to-read type is a must for both the title and the author's name.
- Make sure illustrations and photographs are well done and point to meeting the reader's felt needs.
- Four-color covers sell.
- Make sure you can read the title from across the room.
- Reduce and duplicate your cover in black and white to see how it will reproduce in newspapers, magazines, and marketing material.
- Pay attention to the spine. Your book will usually be shelved spine out, so it needs to make an impression. Make sure the spine reads from top to bottom since this is how books are shelved.

The Back Cover

After the cover, the best way to sell more books is with well-written copy. The perfect title and front cover must motivate buyers to turn the book over in approximately four seconds. Your back cover must begin the process of delivering on the promise that you can meet the reader's felt needs. You might get as many as eight seconds for this crucial step; but if you don't deliver, your book is placed back on the shelf. Amazon.com knows the habits of book buyers. That's why they realized early on that you can sell a book by its cover; you just need to include both the front and the back. Authors who understand the way readers choose books often opt to pay a higher rate to include not only the front and back covers, but several sample pages as well.

What should be included on the back cover? Whatever it is must emphasize benefits, not features. This is the part many authors hate.

It's hard to think of something so personal as a book, something you've invested years to write, something that is a part of you, in marketing terms. You felt called by God to write this exact book, at this exact time. You've created something inordinately valuable that will entertain, heal, soothe, educate, support, or something else of vital importance. Why must it all come down to marketing? Because that's the way it is.

You may not have a marketing degree, and it might remain the least enjoyable part of being a published author; but you can learn how to write back-cover copy that sells your book and doesn't just fill up space. I've had a copy of *Words That Sell* by Richard Bayan since 1987 when I opened my marketing firm in Hawaii. It has proven an even more valuable resource for writing back-cover copy and Web site content. (At the end of this book, I've included a list of helpful books like this one that are available through my online bookstore.)

A Leading Statement or Question

The buyer already knows the title from the front cover. Repeating the title on the back cover is not only redundant, but a waste of space. Instead, making a statement or asking a question that leads back to a need immediately begins the process of telling your reader your book can deliver. Visit libraries, bookstores, and Internet sites to get some examples of statements and questions that have been successful.

A Bulleted List or Synopsis

We're back to benefits versus features. Don't make buyers work to learn why they should buy your book. Bulleted lists of benefits, stated in carefully chosen terms, work well for topic-specific books. A few lines of a plot or riveting dialogue can be included for fiction.

Endorsements

Imagine you've written a book that meets the needs of parents of strong-willed children. Better yet, imagine Dr. James Dobson of Focus on the Family has read your book and calls it the best book on the subject of parenting strong-willed children since his book on the same subject. Where will you put that review?

The answer is obvious: on the back cover where people will be sure to see it, even if they don't open the book before buying a copy. Endorsements sell more books than any other piece of back-cover copy.

Later in this book, I'll talk about how to get endorsements and reviews; but even as you are writing your book, think about who will endorse it. Include top professionals in your field and readers who have benefited from your book. If you're writing fiction, seek a well-known author who writes in your genre and readers who enjoyed your book. Sometimes comments from celebrities and media personalities might be helpful additions. For the back cover, try to get four or five solid endorsements from recognizable names. You can also include more in the first few pages, along with additional endorsements.

For most potential buyers, there's security in buying a book that someone they respect has recommended. As long as I can remember, Crest toothpaste has used the line, "nine out of ten dentists choose Crest," in their commercials. Did they say it was my dentist who recommended it? No, but the implication is there: Because you trust your dentist, you can trust Crest. The same thing goes for book endorsements.

Author's Bio and Photo

There's no law that says your bio and photo must be on the back cover. When deciding what to add, ask yourself this one question: Will adding this help people understand that this book will answer their questions, solve their problems, or meet their needs? Normally, a one- or two-line bio and a small photo can be included on the back cover. A more detailed bio and a larger photo can always be included in the back of the book, rather than taking up valuable back-cover space.

Can you see why I said that the title, cover, and back cover are the cornerstones in building a great book? Thinking marketing before, during, and after you write your book is the number one strategy to getting your book to the people who need it.

Featured Authors

Eva Marie Everson	www.evamarieeverson.com
Linda Fulkerson	www.theprodigaldaughter.com
Sharon Jaynes	www.gospelcom.net/p31
Caron Loveless	www.caronloveless.com
Janet Holm McHenry	www.janetmchenry.com
Brenda Nixon	www.parentpwr.com
Kari West	www.gardenglories.com

Chapter

Insulate Your Structure
Endorsements, Reviews, Speaking Platforms

Start by doing what's necessary, then what's

possible, and suddenly you are doing the

impossible.

—St. Francis of Assisi

Once Homer Smith agreed to build the chapel for Mother Superior in *Lilies of the Field,* he cleared the site. In the book publishing world, clearing the site means choosing your book's topic, doing an outline, starting your research, and writing the best book possible. In construction, once the site is cleared, a strong foundation must be built. For you this means choosing your title; designing your cover, or at least thinking about it; and writing your back-cover copy.

The final part of your book's site preparation includes getting endorsements and reviews and coming up with your speaking platforms, if that's a gift you have. These are all important if you want to reach as many people as possible with the message God has given you. At this stage, many authors get nervous. They don't have a clue how to get endorsements or book reviews; and, besides, they don't know key people. If they choose to self-publish, they might even feel more awkward about this part of the business.

Before Homer arrives on the scene, Mother Superior manages to get some bricks donated for her cause. Before long, the bricks are gone; and she promises to somehow get more, even when there is no visible means of getting them. That type of blind faith is what you need when it comes to getting reviews and endorsements. Mother Superior prayed about the bricks, but she also wrote letters asking for donations; and as she wrote, she continued praying. The first step in obtaining what you need is prayer. Like Mother Superior, you should also be bold and ask for what you need. It's amazing how many wonderful, influential people are happy to help, particularly in the Christian market.

Endorsements

Like you, your customer has a limited amount of disposable income to spend on books. Endorsements sell books. If potential buyers are going to part with some of those dollars, they want a guarantee of sorts that a book will meet their need. Seeing names they recognize and trust, or even seeing favorable comments from readers they aren't familiar with, increases their security. Will good endorsements make up for a weak title, an innocuous cover, and bad writing? Of course they won't. But a solid number of excellent endorsements will enhance what you've already done correctly.

Endorsements are an effective part of your back-cover copy, but they can also be featured in the first few pages of your book. They can be used on your Web site; in promotional literature, such as press kits, postcards, and newsletters; as well as in future books you will write.

Take a look at a few fiction and nonfiction books in your collection. Most of them will have more than one endorsement, and each one featured might say something unique. You'll want to think about your book's different features and try to get those endorsing the book to mention as many different ones as possible in their comments. In my letter or e-mail asking for endorsements, I've specified several benefits I'd like to see mentioned and I have been pleased with the results. Before asking, make sure the benefit is obvious.

The best way to get endorsements is to ask for them. It sounds far too simple, and some endorsements might come through other channels; but it really does work. You have to remember that each time an expert's name is included in a new book, that's exposure for him or her. Many people genuinely want to help authors achieve their goals. I've been asked to endorse books; and if the book is about a topic I feel confident about, such as Huntington's Disease or the Internet, I typically agree to take a look. I've been tapped for several novel endorsements; and if it's a genre I enjoy and routinely read, I say yes. What I don't agree to do is endorse a book about a topic where my name is meaningless or is something I don't read, such as science fiction.

T. Suzanne Eller, author of *Real Teens, Real Stories, Real Life* (RiverOak), explains her process of getting endorsements: "The first question you need to ask is who are people that connect with your readers? You can start locally, regionally and nationally. I chose several national speakers, bands, and authors who ministered to the same audience that I hoped to reach with my book. Then I began my research.

"I looked up their organizations in Google.com; and after finding the organization's address or e-mail address, I approached them gently. If they were unable to read it, I thanked them and let it drop. If they were interested, I sent them a copy by mail with a cover letter."

Suzanne had great success in garnering name endorsements. "Most were very gracious. If they were unable to do so, they shared that fact. Others bent over backward, but it was because this was a project that they believed was intriguing or would be a good tool of ministry. I will always be thankful for those busy people who shared their time with me."

Suzanne makes a few important points all authors should remember. These are busy people, and we can't waste their time. She did her homework by asking people who already had a ministry to her same target market; the synergy was there, so she increased her odds of success. She diligently did the work needed to find contact information and continues to be thankful to those who graciously supported her book.

I went about my review process in much the same way with all of my books. When you write for a niche audience, it's easier to find others who will be well-known by your readers. Don't be afraid to start at the top and work your way down from there.

I do a book proposal for every book I write or sometimes don't write. It's a well-known fact that publishers don't buy books as much as they buy book proposals. Before I choose to invest my money in an idea of my own, I do a proposal. If I can't convince myself of the viability of the book, then why should I think I can write one that will meet the needs of a group of readers? A book proposal will always have a marketing section that includes possible or probable endorsements.

When I did the proposal for *WriterSpeaker.com*, I knew I needed both Christian and secular influencers because the book was for both groups. I looked for people who were well-known in the publishing and speaking industry. Dan Poynter has long worn the title of self-publishing expert extraordinaire. I knew a nod from him would sell many copies. Sally Stuart is as recognizable as any other name in Christian publishing, so I wanted her comments as well.

Sometimes it's not the names of people as much as their companies or who they are associated with that will sell books. I had contributed a story to a book by Jennifer Basye Sander a couple of years before I wrote *WriterSpeaker.com*. Jennifer also happens to be the co-author of *The Complete Idiot's Guide to Getting Published* (Alpha Books). This book series is now a household name, and I wanted that name on the back of my book.

After compiling my list of names and addresses, I sent galleys to them. Only one person declined because he would be out of the country. I was thrilled and, like Suzanne, thankful with the response.

With *Portraits of Huntington's* I did everything, including sending the manuscript, by e-mail. I targeted the executive directors of every English-speaking Huntington's association in the world. To that illustrious group, I added the editor of a national magazine for caregivers, a genetic counselor from a major university, a nurse consultant with the Family Caregiver Alliance, and a well-known fundraiser for the cause.

Every person agreed to look at the book, and I sent the manuscript as a Word attachment. They all read the book and sent back their reviews in less than a month. The three directors in Great Britain enjoyed the book so much they asked if I would be willing do a speaking tour in England, Scotland, and Ireland. On that all-expense-paid trip, I ministered to a number of people, enjoyed myself immensely, made great connections, and ultimately sold enough books to pay for half my initial printing.

Invariably, some endorsements arrive too late to be included in the actual book. Thank those who sent them and use these, along with the others, in your promotional material and on your Web site. My final word on endorsements is this: Paid endorsements are not acceptable.

Book Reviews

Book reviews are similar to endorsements in that they are keys in selling books. The cost of a book review is the book, the press kit, and your time. That's much less costly than an advertisement and more effective. An ad says, "I might be good, but someone paid for me to be included." A book review tells readers, "This is a great book, and no one paid anyone anything to say it."

There are two types of reviews. First is the prepublication review published for "the trade," consisting of wholesalers, bookstores, and libraries. These reviews tell the trade what books are coming before the buying public reads the postpublication reviews in newspapers, magazines, and on Web sites. The trade will place orders based, in large part, on the reviews they read in their trade journals. Because influential reviewers receive over one hundred galleys each day, you'll want to make it impossible for them to turn your book away.

Christian Retailing, Publishers Weekly, and other magazines that do prepublication reviews will want to receive galleys at least four months prior to your publication date. These are advance copies that are produced before the book is available to the general public. One way to handle advance copies is to print the entire run of your book and place an "Advance Review Copy" sticker on the front cover of those you are sending out for prepublication reviews. Remember, once you start selling your book, the review copies you send out are no longer advance copies.

The first step in getting reviews is to develop a list of reviewers. At the end of this chapter, you'll find several sources to locate both Christian and secular book review markets.

Getting a self-published book reviewed by a periodical like *Publishers Weekly* or *The New York Times* is incredibly difficult. It can happen, and certainly you should try; but don't get your hopes up too high. Local papers and magazines might be a more realistic place to expect reviews, though nothing is guaranteed.

Carol Forseth is the self-published author of *Gentile Girl: Living with the Latter-day Saints* (Crossroads). She not only got the local reviews she was hoping for, but she managed to get a review in *Publishers Weekly Religion BookLine* and a review and news story in *CBA Marketplace.*

Carol chose to self-publish to be able to launch her book in conjunction with the 2002 Winter Olympics in Salt Lake City. Once she wrote *Gentile Girl,* her story of a Baptist girl attending predominantly Mormon Brigham Young University, she started Crossroads Press. Her book was released January 2, six weeks before the Olympics.

Carol said, "I followed all the rules. I sent a galley three months before the book was out. About six weeks later, I sent a note and SASE postcard, making sure the reviewer received it. She sent the card back saying it wasn't going to be reviewed. [After that note] I got an e-mail from *PW* [*Publishers Weekly*], saying they'd decided to do a roundup of Mormon-related books for the Olympics; but they'd recycled all the January books, and could I send another one. I put a finished copy in that day's priority mail, and e-mailed the editor the press release, book review, and even an author "interview" I'd written for myself.

In Carol's case, she had a topical book. Since the Olympics were being held in Salt Lake City, that was the hook she needed to get people to do more than toss aside her book and press kit. Thanks to the reviews, Family Christian Bookstores ordered 400 copies, leading to signing with Riverside Distributors.

Besides timing and the right topic, persistence has played a big part in Carol's success. "Catching the wave of publicity with the Olympics really helped. Because the book is the story of a Baptist girl at BYU, I wanted to hit the Baptist market. I got some names of people in LifeWay stores but kept getting no for an answer. On that one I just wouldn't take no for an answer."

Carol continued contacting people and sending review copies— with the help of a persistent Baptist pastor. She started at the top and worked her way down and finally got a call from a book buyer with an order a couple of weeks before the Olympics. From there she persisted and got a much-needed review in *Baptist Press* to help LifeWay sales.

"Doing all the right things doesn't necessarily work, but it gives God room to work. For *Gentile Girl*, it was timing and, of course, the wind of the Holy Spirit blowing as I madly rowed my little boat."

The second type of review is obviously postpublication. This is an ongoing process and part of the word-of-mouth marketing your book must have to do well. In addition to the review venues listed at the end of this chapter, use *Christian Writers' Market Guide* and *Writer's Market* to find magazines related to your topic. If you write for children, you might want to focus on the *Children's Writer's & Illustrator's Market*. John Kremer, author of *1001 Ways to Market Your Book*, has a number of useful reports to help you locate appropriate reviewers. He also has a free online newsletter that usually features different newspapers and the appropriate editor for each section. You can find that information yourself by going to newspaper Web sites.

Look at your local newspapers and free papers as excellent places to send your book. They often feature a hometown author, which works well when you do a local book signing. When bookstores know there will be a review of your book in the local paper, they are more likely to invite you to do a signing.

There are an increasing number of online review opportunities. Even as you're writing your book, surf the Web and bookmark sites related to your topic. For example, you'll find reviews of my Huntington's Disease books on Web sites for national associations, support groups, medical centers, and other places where those dealing with this disease find support. Caregiving, related diseases, and other neurological Web sites have also reviewed my books.

Of course, there is an impressive array of online bookstores from Amazon.com to those specializing in niche topics. I'll discuss online bookstores later; but if your book is carried online, ask friends and readers to place reviews on the lesser-known sites, as well as on Amazon.com and Christianbooks.com.

Whether you're trying to get a pre or postpublication review, you'll need to do more than send a book. Try to find the name, or at least the department, that is the obvious choice to review your book. Smaller papers sometimes have only one book review editor, while larger ones have an editor for health, cookbooks, business, religion, etc. Address your correspondence to the right editor to increase your chances of getting a review.

I will cover press releases in greater detail later in this book, but for now note the need to include one with any book you want reviewed.

Once your book is released, the review process doesn't stop. It doesn't matter how old your book is because there is always someone who hasn't heard of or read it yet. Nothing sells a book like a solid review, and every review means possible sales from a segment of your audience you have no other way to reach.

Eva Marie Everson did an outstanding job of getting reviews for her first novel, *Shadow of Dreams,* co-authored with G. W. Francis Chadwick, and has had even greater success with the sequel, *Summon the Shadows.* "I have several e-mail lists—friends, family, and ministry. To build a review list for Amazon.com and Christianbook.com, I sent an e-mail message to these lists, asking for those who would be willing to read the book and review it at these two sites. I also asked that the readers/reviewers be willing to contact their favorite bookstores and libraries, and tell their families and friends about the book. In return, they would receive a free, signed copy of my first novel, *Shadow of*

Dreams. I did ask, however, that they not respond to the request unless they were lovers of suspense/intrigue fiction."

Eva Marie's strategy was successful because of several factors. She asked people who were already familiar with her ministry and her as a person. All writers should begin compiling a database of family, friends, and ministry partners as soon as they decide to write a book. People are often excited about knowing a writer and will cheerfully review books by people they know. She gave people an autographed copy of her book as a thank you, and she qualified her reviewers by making sure they enjoyed the type of book she had written.

"Nearly sixty people responded immediately; the first fifty were sent the book. Out of those fifty, about half responded to the Web sites as we'd asked (though every single one contacted me personally to let me know how much they had enjoyed the book)."

Eva Marie built on that success with her second book. "I contacted several authors and influential people I knew who had read the first book, asking for a review of *Shadow of Dreams* for the front pages of *Summon the Shadows.* The reviews were wonderful! These authors were, obviously, sent a complimentary signed copy of *Summon the Shadows* as well."

Here's a copy of the note the authors included in each of the books they sent to people who agreed to read and review their books:

> In appreciation of your review for *Shadow of Dreams,* the authors and publisher of book two in the Shadow series would like to give you this complimentary copy of *Summon the Shadows.* We hope you enjoy it as much, if not more, than the first book and that you will review it for us at Amazon.com and Christianbook.com. That done, would you contact your local library and ask them to carry it? Your favorite bookstore and tell them "they simply must!" Then tell all your friends (make them get their own copies). Finally, would you pray for us, that God continues to use us in this ministry He has chosen for us? We will certainly pray for you, too!

Many authors have difficulty with the concept of giving books away. To them, a book that is given away is lost revenue. If your book is well written, the opposite is true. Getting people to review your book has the potential for increased sales.

For years I was a sales rep for various companies. One employer stressed the "rule of two hundred." Studies had shown that most people have about two hundred people in their circles of family and friends. They polled caterers and funeral homes and discovered that the average wedding and funeral each had roughly two hundred people in attendance. What this means is that at any given time, from early adulthood to death, most people have at least two hundred people they know well enough to attend their weddings or their funerals. What it also means is that each book you give away has the possibility to get you a great review and that reviewer knows at least two hundred people who might be interested in your book.

The value of a good review is greater than any money you might earn from a sale. That doesn't mean you give all your books away; but it does mean that giveaways—whether to friends or family or as raffle or door prizes—should be looked at as a key marketing strategy.

If your book is being published through a royalty house, you'll want to coordinate your efforts with its marketing department. Compile your list of influential people and ask your publisher to send them a review copy.

At the end of this chapter is a list of book review Web sites, followed by an excellent article by Jim Cox of Midwest Book Review, "How the Book Review System Works," which will help you further understand this important marketing tool.

Speaking Platforms

Each book, particularly nonfiction, has at least one topic that is suitable as a speaking platform. Even speaking about how and why you became an author is interesting to most people. Any book on marketing you pick up will suggest speaking as a way to sell books. While it's true that many books are sold through a speaking platform, public speaking may not be for everyone.

You might be like me and know you are called to speak. When I do an outline and ultimately write the book, I keep speaking in mind. All of my books have several chapters that can easily be used as the basis of a class or a speech. Crafting my talks from the book's contents allows me to refer to my book in a nonsales way and pique people's interest. Because I keep speaking topics in mind when I write my books, I typically sell to 60 percent or more of my audience each time I speak.

That said, there are many, many authors who are not called to speak. Sadly, there are too many people, both in and out of churches, who are miserable and doing a terrible job in their speaking "ministry." When we are called into a speaking ministry, it's not just to sell books. God wants us to reach a hurting world. Period. He uses writers and speakers and musicians and counselors and any number of servants to reach that world. God will always equip and anoint those He truly calls to serve. He will most likely stretch our comfort levels, like He did with Moses who was filled with reasons that he shouldn't be the one to serve, but He will always be there for us.

Jill Lord, author of *Snuggles with God: Big Hugs for Little Hearts* (Honor), doesn't have a speaking ministry; but she is exactly where God wants her. "When my book came out, I dreamed great dreams for this book. I would give it to orphanages, hospitals, sick people, lonely people. I called orphanages, hospitals, homeless shelters, etc. I was going to get this book out to people who couldn't otherwise afford it."

Jill soon found out that her plan wasn't necessarily God's plan. "Every one of my plans fell through. Not one succeeded. None. All the plans fell through for 'freak' reasons. God sure got my attention. I gave it over to Him, which I thought I had already done, until my plans got in the way. Slowly but surely, opportunities arose to send my books on mission trips. It was a quieter, less grandiose means; but I truly believe it was God's way."

She continues with something we all need to remember, sometimes on a daily basis. "I've learned the hard way. I've learned that God's ways are best. We have to believe if our books, articles, whatever, were inspired, God will complete what He set out to do—big marketing strategies or not—which is especially comforting for those of us who are not public speakers."

The key to successful book marketing is to explore as many ways as possible to sell books. Then we need to understand what we do best and merge the two together. When we do so, we use our unique gifts to create a winning promotional plan. Of course, executing the plan with excellence is what we are all called to do.

I'll talk more about speaking in chapter seven. There are ways that people can improve on their abilities, but some writers just aren't speakers. As you create your marketing plan, look inside your book for possible speaking platforms, which include article topics. While you might not be called to speak, you're obviously called to write; and a well-written article, seen by thousands, can be as effective a marketing tool as speaking.

Featured Authors

Brenda Nixon	www.parentpwr.com/
Eva Marie Everson	www.evamarieeverson.com
Carol Forseth	www.gentilegirl.com
Caron Loveless	www.caronloveless.com
Janet Holm McHenry	www.janetmchenry.com
Kari West	www.gardenglories.com
Linda Fulkerson	www.theprodigaldaughter.com
Sharon Jaynes	www.gospelcom.net/p31
T. Suzanne Eller	www.daretobelieve.org

Christian Book Reviews

CBA	www.cbaonline.org
Christian Library Journal	www.christianlibraryj.org
Christian Retailing	www.christianretailing.com
Church Libraries	www.eclalibraries.org/ magazine.htm
Crosshome.com	www.crosshome.com
This Christian Life	www.thischristianlife.com

General Book Reviews

BookPage®	www.bookpage.com
Bookzone Pro	www.bookzonepro.com/reviewers
Bookideas.com	www.bookideas.com
Booklist	www.ala.org/booklist/index.html
Book Reporter	www.bookreporter.com
BookReview.com	www.bookreview.com
Book Review Cafe	www.bookreviewcafe.com
Book Review Club	www.bookreviewclub.com
Fearless Books	www.fearlessbooks.com
The Horn Book	www.hbook.com/magreview.shtml
Kirkus Reviews	www.kirkusreviews.com
Midwest Book Review	www.midwestbookreview.com
NonfictionReviews.com	www.nonfictionreviews.com
Publishers Weekly	www.publishersweekly.com

SCBWI Publications   www.scbwi.org/pub.htm
School Library Journal   http://slj.reviewsnews.com/index.
       asp?publication=slj
Women on Writing   www.womenonwriting.com

Online Bookstores

1Bookstreet.com   www.1bookstreet.com
AllBookstores.com   www.allbookstores.com
Amazon.com   www.amazon.com
Barnes and Noble   www.bn.com
Berean Christian Bookstore   www.berean.com
Books-a-Million   www.booksamillion.com
Christianbooks.com   www.christianbooks.com
Indigo Books   www.chapters.indigo.ca
Parable Christian Stores   www.parable.com
WordsWorth Books   www.wordsworth.com

How the Book Review System Works

by Jim Cox, Midwest Book Review

A good review placed in the hands of the reading public by a competent reviewer is the most effective and least expensive publicity/promotion instrument available to the independent publisher. But the chances of getting your book reviewed can be drastically reduced if you do not understand what you are up against and do not take steps to improve your odds.

The Midwest Book Review receives approximately 50 books a day, Monday through Saturday. That works out to around 1,500 titles a month. I encourage PMA [Publishers Marketing Association] members to identify themselves as such when they submit their titles for review because Midwest Book Review has a policy of bumping small presses and PMA members to the top of the review list–a significant step when the line is 1,500 titles long!

Other book review publications or programs (with the possible exception of The Independent Publisher) do not have a deliberate policy of giving preference to the small press publisher, so it's always important to keep track of those reviewers for whom your book (by virtue of its theme, subject or publisher status) will have an edge over the other submissions received by that reviewer.

It's my job as the editor-in-chief with a roster of 38 reviewers to produce four library newsletters and two book review magazines each month, a weekly half-hour television show and a monthly short-wave radio broadcast. It is also my responsibility to initially sort out the books submitted for review and to make the review

---

James A. Cox is the Editor-in-Chief of the Midwest Book Review. He publishes four monthly library newsletters; five monthly on-line book review magazines; produces an on-air book review column for KNLS radio which is transmitted to 124 countries; writes "The Jim Cox Report" which is a monthly column of observations with respect to small press publishing concerns, questions and issues; maintains a massive website dedicated to writing, publishing, and reading; and supervises seventy-six volunteer reviewers.

assignments, collect the reviews from the assigned reviewers, and then edit them into our publications and/or programming.

I post these reviews on thematically appropriate Websites, newsgroups, and online bookstores, and I send them (by computer disk) to be included on an interactive cd-rom for corporate, academic, and public library systems. Incidentally, this Internet business takes one full working day each month to accomplish. Then I must send a tear sheet or review script and a cover letter to the publisher, notifying him or her that the title was featured and the various venues in which the review appeared. This process takes about eight working days to accomplish.

Of the more than 1,500 titles a month received, about half (750) are assigned, and only around 450 are reviewed. That's about one-third of the total submitted. Compared with other book review publications or programs, that is a significantly high ratio of books sent to books reviewed.

Those that did not make the initial cut for review failed to be assigned because they either came from the major presses and got bumped in favor of small presses, came in the form of galleys and we only consider finished books, had truly inferior covers, were subjects for which other titles filled that month's quota of a given topic, were missing publicity releases, had been flawed in the printing/book production process, or were damaged in transit (The post office seems to have improved lately, but still, about 1 in 20 book packages sustains some degree of damage, ranging from minor to catastrophic).

Those books that make the cut for review assignment but for which no reviews were eventually published fall into one of the following categories:

1. The assigned book reviewer determined that the book was substantially flawed and that he or she could not honestly recommend it to its intended readership. One thing that distinguishes the Midwest Book Review from other book review publications is that we only publish or broadcast reviews that recommend books to the intended readerships (as well as bookstore retailers, librarians, parents, and teachers).

    These disqualifying flaws could be in the quality of writ-

ing, the organization (especially for nonfiction), or the production values (e.g. binding so poor that it would not hold
up—important for children's hard covers), or the availability
of other books covering the same topic that are better or
more comprehensively written (again, especially important
with respect to nonfiction).

2. The reviewer submitted a review that was flawed (in the
judgment of the editor-in-chief). Anyone can volunteer to
become a reviewer and be assigned a book to see if he or she
can write a readable and informative review—it's actually a
fairly skilled proposition. Some folk don't have a knack for
writing reviews.

3. The reviewer never turns in a review (in which case it is their
last assignment). Some people don't appreciate how much
work is involved until they try to write a review. For others,
becoming a reviewer was just a passing fancy that passed all
to quickly.

There is a traditional agreement between the publisher and
the reviewer. It goes like this:

1. Publishers have the right to submit their book(s) for review
consideration as long as they follow the submission process
as set out by the reviewer (galleys vs. finished books, appro-
priateness of book's subject matter, publication date deadlines, etc.).

2. Reviewers have the right to accept or reject a submission on
any grounds they deem sufficient. These could include such
considerations as too many submissions to consider them
all; poorly written or defectively published; insufficient or
poorly organized publicity release and/or media kit; inappropriate content; inappropriate publication date; too many
books on a particular theme; a better book on a given topic
is already in hand; the reviewer is having a bad hair day; etc.,
ad nauseam.

3. The publisher has the right to a follow-up contact with the
reviewer after submitting a book for review to ascertain three
things: 1) that the book arrived safely; 2) the status of the

book with respect to the review process; and 3) if the reviewer needs any additional information.

4. Once a book is reviewed, the publisher has a right to a copy of the review, provided by the reviewer (or his/her editor). There is no corresponding obligation to inform the publisher that a book has been rejected for review—the absence of any tear sheet is deemed sufficient to establish that outcome.

5. The publisher has the automatic authority to utilize the review, in part or in whole, in publicity/promotion/advertising/marketing material for the book. (This is the quid-pro-quo for having provided a free review copy.) I appreciate publishers who notify me of any typos they may spot in a review. Even with two eyes proofing and a spell checker checking, a correctly spelled wrong word still manages to get through now and then. Once I even used a book's subtitle as the title—and to this day I don't know how I managed to do that! Although it is too late for those corrections to be made in the newsletters, they can still be made in the magazines (Internet Bookwatch and Children's Bookwatch) quite easily—and should be inasmuch as the reviews will be up on our website for five months.

The most common reasons for a book's failure to be reviewed are as follows:

1. It was not submitted according to the submission guidelines and preferences of a particular book review publication or program. For example, galleys were sent when only the finished books are considered—or finished books were sent when only galleys are considered.

2. The book subject was inexpertly handled by the author.

3. The book is flawed—either in the writing or as a published entity.

4. Insufficient information was included with the book to complete a review (I can't tell you how often important information is missing, such as a price, publisher address, 800 numbers, and publicity releases.

5. Space or time limitations prevent its use. For example, I'm doing a poetry column, and I've got room for 10 books. Thirteen excellent titles were submitted, but I don't have enough space to use them all. Sometimes it is as raw as the flip of a coin; sometimes it's easier. For instance, if two books were from Simon & Schuster and one was from Penguin Putnam, those would be bumped because our policy of preferring small presses would kick in and make an automatic cut for me.

Good book reviewers always send out tear sheets to the publishers. Mediocre ones will if prodded. Scam artists never do. Keep good records on the review copies you send out. If you send a book to a given book reviewer or publication and it is reviewed and a tear sheet is sent, add the reviewer to your "highly valuable" resource file for future publishing projects. Send a thank you note; name your first born after him or her. When submitting your next title, customize your cover letter to note how much you appreciated the previous review and that you are especially pleased to be submitting this second (or third or fourth, etc.) book.

If your book was reviewed but you had to prod the reviewer for a tear sheet, note that situation and put it in your "I've got to put a little extra effort in the follow-up with these guys" file. But you still have a useful resource so don't lose track of it.

If your book has fallen into a book review black hole never to be heard of again, consider the following before writing them off:

1. Did you do your homework and find out what their submission standards were and if there were a specific person to whom it should have been addressed to?
2. Having their submission guidelines, did you follow them?
3. Was your book thematically appropriate for that particular Book Review?
4. Did you submit your book during an appropriate time of year to maximize your chances for getting attention? This is extremely important for small presses trying to get the notice of the big guys such as Publishers Weekly, Library Journal, The New York Times Book Review, and Bloomsbury.

5. Did you read Jim Cox's article on How to Spot a Phony Book Reviewer?
6. Did you do the ten-working-day-follow-up?

If you answered yes to all, then write it off to your publicity/promotion overhead and move on. You may get some serendipity out of the submission later—it has been known to happen. But in any event, it's how the game is played and a part of your operating overhead. Put that particular reviewer in your "only if there are enough copies in my promotional budget to spare a title will I consider these guys the next time around" file.

If you answered no to any of the questions, you may want to rethink your submission strategy (which is a part of your overall marketing plan for the title) and consider resubmitting or just determining to do better with that book reviewer next time.

And, of course, there is the third list you should be keeping—the one containing book reviewers that are not appropriate for the kind of book(s) you publish, the scam artists, and reviewers or that have submissions guidelines so stringent that bothering with them isn't worth your time.

Remember that prepublication book review publications such as Publishers Weekly and Library Journal are looking for reasons to disqualify your submission, to prune their 5000+ incoming titles a month to a manageable size—and resulting list is not going to be anywhere near one-third of those submitted.

Featured Resources

Midwest Book Review	www.midwestbookreview.com
Publishers Marketing Association	www.pma-online.org
"How to Spot a Phony Book Reviewer"	www.midwestbookreview.com/bookbiz/advice/phony.htm

Section Two

Choosing the Right
Tools and Materials

Power Tools
Creating Winning Press Kits and Press Releases

Four steps to achievement: Plan purposefully.

Prepare prayerfully. Proceed positively. Pursue

persistently.

—William A. Ward

Imagine yourself in the middle of building a house and running out of bricks. You live in an area where lumber is not plentiful, and you wonder how you will complete your project. You have a vision of that finished structure, yet without materials you are unable to continue.

That's exactly how Mother Superior felt in *Lilies of the Field*. She knew God had called her to build a chapel. She now had a contractor, albeit a reluctant one. She prayed and wrote letters and prayed some more, yet for a while, she couldn't see God's provision.

We would all love to be best-selling authors and get our books to millions of people. We would be thrilled with an all-expenses paid, multicity book tour; appearances on major talk shows; and book reviews in the top media outlets. Some authors get all that and more, and God uses their books in ways they never anticipated. And then there are the rest of us. If you're reading this book, you're probably one of "us." You don't have a publisher who will expend a huge amount on promoting your book, and you certainly don't have that kind of money yourself. But that doesn't mean God won't use you and your book in incredible ways.

Mother Superior never did get enough bricks to complete her chapel, but it was finished despite the shortfall. In fact, what resulted was a building far more suited to the arid desert. Homer Smith's helpers used affordable and available material that had been used for generations, adobe. They used their feet to mix a substance that ultimately honored God and served the people.

Think of press tours and royal treatment as the best steel beams and glass available to build an earthquake-proof skyscraper. To this, add renowned architects, builders, craftsmen, bulldozers, and other implements; and you're almost guaranteed architectural success.

When it comes to marketing, most of us work with adobe. It doesn't mean we can't be successful in our efforts to serve God and reach people, it means we need to be realistic and choose the tools and materials best suited to our budgets, our audiences, and God's call on our lives.

Media Kits

When I discussed book reviews and endorsements, I mentioned including a press kit with a copy of your galley or book. This is sometimes called a media kit. Besides the obvious copy of your book or galley, what goes into it?

The answer to that question depends on why and where you are sending your kit. If you are sending a book for review, a one-page release, your business card, and the galley or book is all that's needed.

If you're sending a kit to the media in hopes of an interview or a story about you or the book, then you can add more to the kit because this is information people will need to make their decisions. Either way, remember that the media get inundated with media kits every day of the week and have a stack of contenders for that morning drive-time interview or Sunday supplement cover story.

Media kits range from glossy, embossed folders with information printed on high quality letterhead to simple, uncluttered, yet professional and affordable presentations. As long as the inserts are error free and include the essentials, you don't need to spend a lot of money to get attention. You can buy presentation folders at your local office supply store, or you can work through a printer to create a unique look with your name, book title, or cover. Paper Direct and Presskits.com both offer an array of materials you can order online.

Whether you buy off the shelf or create something unusual, what's important is to match your kit to the audience. Are you trying to reach *Dateline?* Then something more impressive might be in order. A more subdued kit could be used for your local Christian television station.

As Christian authors, we are called to share our books with both secular and Christian audiences. A non-Christian reader will often pick up even an overtly Christian book. You never know how God will use your book; but if you don't try to get secular interviews, you are limiting who you can reach. In addition to your Christian media kit, consider having a different kit for secular stations, network shows, etc. You're not compromising your witness, but you're making it easier to get in the door in secular markets.

The media has seen it all. There's little you can send that will impress them besides outstanding writing with an attention-grabbing headline and a high impact lead. They want your story in a concisely told format that makes it easy for them to decide if you are worth their time and reputation to pursue. If what you send them piques their interest, they will contact you. The most important part of your kit is a dynamite press release giving them a reason to open your book and look at any other materials you've sent.

Media kits can include a number of different items, depending on your purpose and who you are targeting. Not all of the following items are required, but here are typical ones to have on hand:

- Presentation folder
- Personalized cover letter
- Press release
- Your galley or book
- Author bio (could also be a separate brochure)
- Photograph (also called a head shot)
- Business card
- One sheet
- Endorsements and reviews
- Speaking topics (if applicable)
- List of suggested questions
- List of articles (about you) and appearances
- Copies of newspaper articles
- Promotional items, such as bookmarks, postcards, and promo cards
- Giveaways

In the next chapter I'll write more about some of these items and give you ideas on where to locate items within your budget.

Press Release

There are different ways to craft a press release, but the one accompanying your book or galley is quite simple. It should include contact information; the title and ISBN number; author's name; number of pages; price; and additional information, such as a toll-free number or Web site.

Write releases in third person and include a concise description of the book. Remember the benefits to your reader on your back cover? These can be included in your press release. This is not the time to brag about you or your book. It is the time to give carefully crafted information that the media can use to decide if they want to give you any press or write a review.

I'll cover how to write a news-oriented release and give an example later in this chapter.

Author's Bio

Your media kit bio will be similar to what is included in your book. It can also be longer, but it should still be written in third person and not appear boastful. This is the time to list appropriate facts and experiences that point to your credibility as the book's author. My bio for both of my Huntington's Disease books points out not only my writing experience, but also the fact that I am a speaker on Huntington's Disease and related topics. That I was a caregiver for someone with this disease is an excellent example of something that has made me credible to the media. You may also list your education and employment history, but only if it is relevant to your book.

Your bio must be tightly written and as brief as possible. It will receive only a glance, so make sure that what you say grabs the reader. Don't overinflate to make yourself sound better, but don't play down your excellence either.

Head Shot

I once had someone tell me I didn't look like a writer when I told her what I did for a living. "What does a writer look like?" I asked. She had no answer except that a writer doesn't look like me. So what does a writer look like? You can clear that up by including a photo in your media kit.

People like to match a face to a name or a book title, so your photograph is often a nice addition to your kit, depending on where it's being sent. A head shot is simply a professional quality photo of you that can be added to your book cover and Web site or featured in newspaper and magazine articles. Head shots can be black and white or color. A five- by seven-inch or four- by six-inch is a good size because the photo can be more easily reduced to a different size if needed. If you start with a smaller photo it can become distorted if someone enlarges it.

Type or write your name and contact information on a label, and affix it to the back. Never write directly on the photo paper because no matter how carefully you write, inevitably indentations will be picked up when reproducing the photo. You may also include a self-addressed, stamped envelope (SASE) with a request to return your photo. Another option is to give a link where an electronic version of your head shot can be downloaded. Many publications prefer working with an actual photo, so find out what the editor wants.

Carefully consider your pose, clothing, and setting when taking a picture that will be representative of how people perceive you. The type of book you've written could help you decide whether to wear a suit or something more representative of your profession or topic. I've seen many photos of doctors wearing lab coats on the books they have authored. If your book is about homeschooling, you might want to go for a more casual, fun look.

Most people hate the way they look in photos, and I'm no exception. I tried having a glamour photo done, and that was a disaster. The photos certainly didn't reflect my topic, profession, or lifestyle! Next I went to two photographers featured in national retail chains and didn't fare any better. I eventually used a professional makeup artist and found an award-winning photographer. I couldn't afford his rates, so I offered to create a Web site in exchange for the photo shoot and an agreed upon number of prints in a variety of sizes. I also got a signed release giving me the copyright. This way anyone can use the photos I send without having to ask for permission or pay an additional fee.

Business Card

A business card offers a quick way for the media to contact you without having to cull through your release or bio. A business card can also be filed for use at a later time if they what you have written is relevant to a story or some other situation.

The same rules apply to business cards as any other piece of promotional material. Keeping it clean and uncluttered with lots of white space helps people read your card. You can use your photo or logo, but less is often more when it comes to such a small piece of paper. Some authors use the backside to list published books or speaking topics.

Office supply stores, such as Office Max, Office Depot, and Staples, sell perforated business cards that can be fed into your laser or inkjet printer. There are a large variety of papers and designs to chose from, and these are quite affordable. Paper Direct is another source for preprinted paper and business cards.

Another way to get affordable business cards is through a company called Vista Print. It offers 250 cards for the cost of shipping, and there are many designs. The only negative side of this offer is that one line of advertising appears on the back of every card.

Eventually you'll want to order business cards, letterhead, and envelopes that match and reflect your personality.

One Sheets

A one sheet is a double-sided sheet that many authors and speakers use to encapsulate their information in one place. Often on glossy or colorful paper that reflects your personality and topic, a one sheet includes your photo, bio, speaking or teaching topics, promotional blurbs, and other information of interest to the media. There are several excellent examples of one sheets on my Web site at www.writers-peaker.com/youcan.html. Printing a few at a time allows you to make changes instantly, rather than waiting until you've used up your stock of 1,000 copies. Color always speaks louder than black and white and is also more expensive. You can print what is called a shell in bulk quantity with only your photo, a header, and any other graphics or words requiring color. Once printed, you can run them through your printer one at a time and send them out as requested or needed.

Book Reviews

You can also include copies of particularly glowing reviews, especially if they are from sources that are well known and respected. Including a review from *Publishers Weekly* or *Christian Retailing* can only help unless it reflects poorly on your book. Then, of course, you wouldn't include that review.

List of Suggested Questions

Remember, your job is to give the media what they need to decide you are the perfect person for a show or column. A list of suggested questions can show producers that you are someone with an interesting story that their audiences will enjoy hearing.

Normally you send a list of questions to television and radio media and not to newspapers and magazines. You can reference the available list and offer it if editors would like to see it, but they often will want to ask their own questions.

With so many guests, don't be surprised if a producer and, certainly, an on-air personality don't read your book or even your questions before interviewing you. This fact makes the questions you write even more important and will help ensure you have solid interview content.

The suggested questions should point readers to your book without being pushy or overly commercial. Your answers will drive the interview and keep it lively, which is a must. Your book's topic will dictate the questions, as well as anything unique or memorable about you.

It's a good idea to include several questions on three or four topics. When preparing questions for specific media, listen or watch their shows to learn their approach. Are some interviewers only looking for the sensational? Do they try to embarrass you? Are they calm and unhurried and willing to spend time helping you develop your answers?

Try and tie your suggested questions into current news and topics of interest. Huntington's is an incurable, genetic disease that impacts people's lives in many ways. I have questions that can lead to discussions about genetic testing, health care, insurance discrimination, family planning, abortion, suicide, assisted suicide, caregiving, stem-cell research, gene therapy, and other issues in the news. I've done my homework and have facts as well as stories in my book that I can give as examples when answering the questions.

Nonfiction books are naturals for suggested questions, but fiction authors need to prepare a list too. You must be informative and entertaining, so make sure to present questions that will help, not hinder, the interviewer.

Wendy Lawton, author of *The Tinker's Daughter* and *Courage to Run* (Moody), has an excellent set of possible interview questions she has allowed me to share with you. I'll write more about e-mail signatures later, but part of Wendy's includes a tag line that beautifully illustrates what she does as an artist. "Telling stories in porcelain; Painting pictures with words" is helping Wendy create her personal brand. Hopefully, reading her questions and abbreviated answers will give you ideas for your own set of questions.

Wendy Lawton's Possible Interview Questions

1. I see that you are a writer and a doll maker. What do these two professions have to do with each other? (It's all about telling stories.)

2. Your books are for girls in late grammar school, early junior high—is that the same age group that enjoys your dolls? (The dolls are collector dolls ranging in price from $500 to an all-time high of $11,000. They are for adult collectors mostly—just like the books will be enjoyed by "girls" of all ages.)

3. Your books are about girls right out of the pages of history. Do girls today find a girl like Mary Bunyan, who lived in the 17th century, relevant to life in the third millennia? (Surprisingly, yes. Mary was born profoundly blind and yet history records her can-do attitude…)

4. You cover Harriet Tubman's life from the age of 6 to the age of 13. That was before her work in the underground railroad. She was still in slavery at the time. (Harriet Tubman already took a stand by the time she was 13…)

5. So, your theme is girl heroes of the faith. How important are heroes to kids these days? (They love to read the stories, but more than ever kids need heroes who do not have super powers, who do not use guns to solve their problems and even more importantly, who choose to act heroically when they are still children—just like the reader.)

6. How does a child get to be a hero? (Interesting studies over the past 20 years, notably the ones done by Ervin Staub…[explain study briefly].)

7. So Staub thinks that empathy is the most important trait in children who act heroically. Is there anything we can do to help our children learn empathy? (There are several things we can do…)

8. One of the things you mention is not to shield our children from hardship. What do you mean by that? (I don't mean we should give them more than they can handle; but through service, through reading, through watching us, let them learn to respond to those in need. One dad I know…)

9. You also say not to expect blind obedience from our children. Isn't that a departure from "Children obey your parents"? (Not at all. Children should obey parents, but parents must encourage the child to exercise discretion. In Staub's study, the older the child, the less chance that they would act heroically because they were afraid of "getting in trouble" for helping without permission…)

10. How did a girl like Harriet Tubman learn to fight the institution of slavery which required blind obedience? (In Harriet Tubman's own words, "'Twas the Lord.")

11. Will there be more books in the series? (Yes. I'm working on a book about Mary Chilton who sailed on the Mayflower…)

Promotional Material

Some authors include postcards or promo cards in their press kits. In the next chapter, I'll discuss promotional items and how to use them; but it is appropriate, depending on where you are sending your press kit, to include these items.

Giveaways

Everyone loves to get something for free, and media professionals are no different. What they don't need is more clutter; so if you're going to add a giveaway to your media kit, choose something memorable that is the perfect tie-in for your book.

Jan Coleman, author of *After the Locusts: Restoring Ruined Dreams, Reclaiming Wasted Years* (Broadman & Holman), includes "locust licks" with the name of the book printed on a label. These clear lollipops, featuring a locust inside, are something most of us have never seen. "I purchased them from a company that makes candy with organically grown insects inside. I bought them by the case to get a cheaper price. They cost about 50 cents each but are worth their weight in bugs!"

I can just see a producer sucking one of Jan's "locust licks" as he reads her press release and scans the book. When I heard about this idea, I immediately thought, *What a fun, creative person she must be, and she'd probably do a great interview.*

Jan shared that "John the Baptist had his [locust] with honey. In Botswana they are a delicacy. They slip a peanut inside and fry them in a wok. In Cambodia they roast them until golden brown. Not only can we survive the locust plagues in our lives, we can feast on them too." Now that's great news and the makings for a wonderful interview.

In the next chapter I'll write more about how to use advertising specialties to sell books.

Crafting an Attention-Grabbing Press Release

By now you should understand how an effective press release can be one of the best promotional tools. Every editor wants to find a good story and it could be in your release. Your release can be looked on as a "prewritten" article, which is good news for editors who don't have enough time to do their jobs. It can also be a starting point to an in-depth article or story if you give them a good enough reason. They want to find something of value in your release, but they have to find it quickly; or they won't find it at all.

The release you send to get a review focuses on the book. For all other releases, remember this one basic rule: A press release must be news.

The media works on deadlines and get mountains of releases, so you need to make yours urgent. Put a date on it, and in big letters across the top write: For Immediate Release. Write attention-getting headlines and copy for all your releases. What you send must be newsworthy, and you'll need to hook the editor right away.

Press releases, even ones that are newsworthy, must be kept short. The one-page rule does have exceptions, but they are few and far between. On my Web site is a press release I recently sent out after a major news story involving Huntington's Disease. It was almost two pages because I needed two pages. However, because it was so timely and had a great tie-in, people responded. I sent the release to six local media outlets, and four answered. All four have done or are in the process of doing a story. Because of the local angle and a specific hook, the release presented reporters with an opportunity to do a timely, interesting story from someone in the community. The fact that I am an author was of less importance than my credibility as a caregiver and being the founder of an online support group for caregivers of those with Huntington's Disease.

Success rates are usually higher with your hometown media. Local stories about hometown heroes are still in vogue. Features departments are always looking for the right material for popular slice-of-life stories.

Just as your articles can be reworked and sent to different markets, so can press releases.

As you craft your release, find an angle and hook the editor. The more work you can do for the editor or producer, the better the odds of that person considering your story. You can direct the focus of your story by the way you slant your release. By now you know all about tight writing with strong verbs and nouns. Of course, you must eliminate passive writing and get rid of adjectives, adverbs, and ambiguous words. In other words, an attention-grabbing press release should be news, be filled with facts without being boring, and showcase your best writing.

There's a temptation to add as much information as you can into each release as if this will be your one and only chance to communicate with this newspaper, radio, or television station. Your job is to present the basics; and once you get the interview, you can elaborate and tell the entire story.

Less is the word in what to include in a cover letter sent with your release. It sounds stark, but editors don't have time for much more. Include in about four short sentences what the story is about, what benefit it will be to the readers, your contact information, and an invitation to read the enclosed press release.

One reason my longer press release worked is because I called the recipients first. I explained the information was two pages and asked for their permission to send it. To increase your chances of getting coverage, you might want to call the intended recipients before you send the release. If you don't hear from them, then call a few days later to make sure they received it. Making first contact by phone will also help you find the appropriate person since, like publishing houses, it's like a game of musical chairs with people coming and going.

Faxing and e-mail have urgency that snail mail will never have. They are also free, except long distance charges if there are any. However, make sure the newspaper accepts faxes and e-mail and what type of attachments the editor will accept. A quick phone call should give you the answer.

There are many services that will blanket the country with your press release for a fee. That's not usually the most effective way to get your release into the hands of someone who will be able to use it. An important rule is to know your target. Consider carefully where to send your release. Know if your information is better suited to the business, sports, or health editor or someone else. Get to know your local paper and who covers what; the same goes for the national media. At the end of this chapter there are several sources for finding media contacts.

It's a good idea to write your press releases in third person and quote yourself. This is a great way to include hard-hitting or informative statements that the media will want to use verbatim in their stories.

Your release might be used as a story with a byline from an editor or reporter. Don't get angry. Just be pleased he decided to run with it. You sent your words out for public release, and there has been no copyright violation in doing so. Press releases are not articles you are submitting for publication with the expectation of another byline. The reader doesn't need to know those were your words.

Timing really is everything. Don't fax a release the day before an event and expect it to receive coverage. Send one early enough to give the editor time to plan. You can always send out another release as the event draws closer. Newspapers will typically have special sections for shopping, health, business, and other topics, in addition to their regular content. Know the deadlines for all the sections because they vary.

Always include, at the top corner of every page, a two- or three-word description of the story, the name and phone number of key contact people (no more than two), the page number, and the release date that is either immediately or "please hold until a specific date."

You may include photos when you mail a release, or include the phrase *photos available on request* with your information at the top of the first page. If you mail it, fold the release so the headline and date are the first thing seen when the editor opens the envelope.

It seems like a little thing, but end your releases with "###" or "30" typed across the center of the page, three lines below the end of your text. If a release has more than one page, type "more," centered at the bottom of the pages preceding the final page.

Several Web sites are listed below that should help you find appropriate media and their addresses, phone numbers, and e-mail addresses. National Religious Broadcasters publishes an annual *NRB Directory of Religious Media* that is key to reaching Christian radio and television stations, Webcasters, talk shows, Christian programs, film and video producers, print and music publishers, agencies, services, suppliers, and other industry contacts. Nonmembers can purchase this directory at a higher price.

Featured Author
Carol Forseth — http://www.gentilegirl.com
Eva Marie Everson — http://www.evamarieeverson.com
T. Suzanne Eller — http://daretobelieve.org
Wendy Lawton — www.wendylawton.com

Featured Resources
One Sheets
Color Printing Central — www.colorprintingcentral.com
One Sheet Samples — www.writerspeaker.com/youcan.html

Business cards
Paper Direct — www.paperdirect.com
Vista Print — www.vistaprint.com

Photo Duplication
Duplicate Photo & Imaging — www.duplicate.com
NRS Publicity Printing — http://my.athenet.net/~nrsprntg/index.html
Photo Factory — www.photofactory.com

Media Searches
50States.com — www.50states.com/news
National Religious Broadcasters — www.nrb.org
Network for Good — www.networkforgood.org/speakout/index.html
CBA — www.cbaonline.org
Christian Library Journal — www.christianlibraryj.org
Christian Retailing — www.christianretailing.com
Church Libraries — ww.eclalibraries.org/magazine.htm
Crosshome.com — hwww.crosshome.com
This Christian Life — www.thischristianlife.com

General Book Reviews
Book Page — www.bookpage.com
Bookzone Pro — www.bookzonepro.com/reviewers
Bookideas.com — www.bookideas.com

Booklist	www.ala.org/booklist/index.html
Book Reporter	www.bookreporter.com
Book Review.com	www.bookreview.com
Book Review Cafe	www.bookreviewcafe.com
Book Review Club	www.bookreviewclub.com
Fearless Reviews	www.fearlessbooks.com
The Horn Book	www.hbook.com/magreview.shtml
Kirkus Reviews	www.kirkusreviews.com
Midwest Book Review	www.midwestbookreview.com
NonfictionReviews.com	www.nonfictionreviews.com
Publishers Weekly	www.publishersweekly.com
SCBWI Publications	www.scbwi.org/pub.htm
School Library Journal	ww.slj.reviewsnews.com/index.asp?publication=slj
Women on Writing	www.womenonwriting.com

Hand Tools
Promotions, Ad Specialties, Book Signings

If you want to succeed, double your failure rate.
—Thomas J. Watson

God can make your book a best-seller with no help from you at all. When that is His plan, nothing can stop Him; but that is not normally the way it works. Even when you are in His will and have written your book because it fits your mission statement, He doesn't usually sell your books for you.

Midway through *Lilies of the Field,* before the people begin to make adobe they eventually used to finish the chapel, Homer runs out of building material. With no material he says it's time to move on because Mother Superior didn't keep her end of the agreement.

She tells Homer, "I failed because I put my faith in people instead of in God."

There's nothing wrong with depending on others to help you with your book promotion. God has given you specific gifts and talents, but there are still many things you don't do well. Thankfully, He has given those gifts to others; and you can seek them out and ask their help.

Because Mother Maria and her nuns were from Germany, Austria, and Hungary, three countries that do not use adobe, she thought the only way to get material was to ask for bricks. She trusted people to provide them; and when they didn't, she thought she couldn't trust people any longer.

With the deluge of new books on the market each year you can see how your book—even when you do all the right things—might not be the one book to get reviewed. And you might not be an author selected to appear on a major talk show. Do you give up and stop trying? Obviously not.

In the last chapter, I discussed the need for a media kit and how to write effective press releases and sample questions. That's a great start, but there are many other ways to market your book.

Printed Promotional Material

In addition to your media kit, you'll want other printed promotional material. If your book has not been printed yet, this is an excellent time to talk to your printer or publisher. Printing extra covers at this point is a minor investment, and those covers can be turned into invaluable promotional items.

If your book is already printed, you don't need to go without these useful items. Printers and specialty companies can print postcards, bookmarks, and other items once you have a copy of your artwork. Check with your local printers; but in the resources section at the end of this chapter, you'll find several sources that might be more affordable Always ask for referrals, and make sure you find out about the quality of their work and how quickly they can deliver.

One of the easiest marketing tips is to begin collecting the names, addresses, and e-mail addresses of every human being you've ever met in your entire life. Family members, co-workers, school friends, church members, and anyone else you've connected with are all possible customers for your book.

Long before your book is out, you'll want to create a database of those names, so you can print mailing labels. Six weeks before my first book arrived, I sent postcards to everyone on my mailing list. Because I didn't know it was possible to get postcards from the publisher and didn't have the good sense to think about it myself, I had my printer produce them on card stock. I made my cards regulation postcard size, so I could pay the less-expensive postage. Rates vary, depending on what is sent and by what method, so check with your post office to compare rates. Both the U.S. and Canadian postal sites are listed at the end of this chapter.

As a writer who also published the book, I was responsible for everything. Thankfully, I chose an excellent publisher who understood the need to get my inventory to me six weeks before my first big convention, so there would be a buzz surrounding the book. I targeted May 1 as the day I'd begin filling advance orders. Amazingly, I began stuffing bubble pack envelopes on May 6.

Thanks to my Web site and postcard mailing, I presold two hundred books at the retail price, which made a great dent in the publishing costs. I went to the Denver Huntington's convention that year, which had eight hundred families in attendance. I sold over six hundred copies, in large part because some attendees had already read the book and recommended that others buy a copy. I also spoke and sang several times at the convention, which increased my sales. Later in this book, I'll discuss speaking as a an effective way to sell books.

After the first book, I knew enough to make sure I had four-color postcards printed for future books at the same time as the cover. The cover was featured on the front of the card and the back had the title, price, ordering information, and my Web site. I requested an earlier shipping date for the postcards and sent them out to my ever-increasing mailing list.

When someone bought *Faces of Huntington's* with a check, or when my fulfillment house sent me customer addresses as part of the quarterly report, I added them to my mailing list. Whenever I had a speaking engagement, I asked people to sign my mailing list, so they could be advised of new products or when I'd be in their area again. When *Portraits of Huntington's* arrived, I had already presold over four hundred copies because of my mailing list and those postcards.

When the publisher shipped my first book, he included 5,000 promotional cards, one for each book I ordered. The cards, printed on the leftover stock when the cover was printed, featured the cover artwork, two reviews, the price in both U.S. and Canadian dollars, and the book packagers toll-free number. As the publisher I wanted to drive traffic to my fulfillment house so I ordered stickers with the new toll-free number and affixed it over the original number.

Now whenever I send out a copy of one my books, I include material on a related book. Even though I don't have any four-color postcards for my first book, I do have promotional cards to include.

I am also able to bring the promotional material and postcards with me to speaking engagements as giveaways on my book table. Having the colorful information often prompts people to order the book once they get home.

I know several authors who place their bookmarks and postcards into their monthly bills and other correspondence. Others leave them in taxis, restaurants, bookstores, airplane seat pockets, and other places people congregate. The cost of each piece ranges from free, if your publisher had the foresight to print them with the cover, to only a few cents if you had them printed yourself. You never know when someone picking up something about your book might decide they need it or give it to a friend who might have a need. Just make sure that ordering information and your Web site is featured. If you don't have a post office box, you might consider getting one to protect your privacy.

Postcards and other printed material come in all shapes and sizes. If you need examples, there are several sample cards from various authors on my Web site.

At the end of this chapter, "Cover Story" by Deborah Raney offers several easy-to-implement ideas of how your cover can be used as postcards, bookmarks, direct-mail pieces, and more. Deborah suggests asking for 3,500 extra covers. If your budget or publisher won't cover that many, don't worry. Some is a lot better than none, so get as many as possible.

Giveaways and Advertising Specialties

Whether you are an author who speaks, a speaker who writes, or someone in between, there are lots of fun ways to promote your book. Thankfully, many of these are inexpensive and easy to implement. All that's needed to use giveaways and advertising specialties is a lot of creativity, a good supplier, and a way to pay for what you need.

For example, to promote her mystery, Nancy Lindquist, author of *Shaded Light* (St. Martins), used small umbrellas or parasols like those placed in drinks in restaurants. "The murder in the book took place in a Japanese garden," she explains. "I thought the parasols looked Japanese. I made little labels with a small picture of the book cover and my Web address, and stuck them on the toothpick endings (after I had cut off the pointy end so no one would be stabbed). They seemed to make an impression."

Nancy built on her parasol idea and used them at various mystery conventions and bookstores. "I put the parasol, along with a Wurther's candy (in a gold foil wrapper—which I thought went with "light"), a bookmark, and a small brochure with the beginning of the book plus a list of my cast of characters, into a small plastic bag. These creative, inexpensive giveaways were picked up by thousands."

In the last chapter, I introduced you to Jan Coleman and her "locust licks." Jan has a passion for those who are trying to reclaim their lives after times of locusts. The title of her book, *After the Locusts: Restoring Ruined Dreams, Reclaiming Wasted Years,* had a built-in opportunity to be creative.

By now you've heard that most publishers spend few promotional dollars on new authors unless they come to the table with a huge following or celebrity status. That might be true in some cases, but you won't know what your publisher is willing to do if you don't ask.

In Jan's case she decided to get some of those promotional dollars. "I approached my editor about coming to the big sales meeting to present my book to the sales force. He said authors rarely ask, but it sounded like a great idea if I'd pay my own way."

Jan used her frequent flier miles for a ticket from her home in California and, through an online travel site, found an affordable, four-star hotel across the street from the publishing house. Once in Nashville she made her pitch. "They gave me twenty minutes to speak about my vision for the book, and at the end I had my husband hand out "locust licks" with the name of the book printed on a label."

Her ending presentation is so good I'll repeat it for those who skimmed the last chapter or who need to be reminded of those locusts times in our lives: "John the Baptist had his [locusts] with honey. In Botswana they are a delicacy. They slip a peanut inside and fry them in a wok. In Cambodia they roast them until golden brown. Not only can we survive the locust plagues in our lives, we can feast on them too."

After the meeting one sales representative came up to Jan and said, "A shameless self-promoter. We love that." Who would have thought anything good would come out of locusts? Jan recalls, "The marketing director asked for a supply of the "locust licks" for the sales force to take to bookstores when they called on them. The head of publicity wanted to put them in every media packet she sent out. I left there not only as an author, but an author with a face, personality, and a message they would not soon forget."

It's easy to think that only those with books at major publishers get any marketing dollars, but it simply isn't true. Jan used an imaginative idea and a little of her time and money to make something happen. She didn't stop with the publisher though. "While I was in Nashville, I stopped in at a radio station that broadcasts to five hundred stations across the country, gave personnel suckers, and they invited me to do a show when the book came out."

This station does only in-house interviews; so using another frequent flier ticket, Jan will stay at the same hotel and do the show. Her publisher didn't set up that major interview; Jan did.

Jan's initial investment would have paid off if the story ended there, but it didn't. "Two weeks later I received a phone call. 'Jan, we've looked at the budget, and there are some marketing dollars left over for you, so we've decided to hire an outside publicist. Any preference?' I'm certain this decision was a direct result of my visit to the publishing house and my eagerness to copromote this book. The trip was well worth the cost in the added attention and marketing dollars that have come my way."

After the Locusts is now in its second printing. With Jan's enthusiasm and willingness to make her book a success, she is reaching people who need to read God's word.

Jan is looking for new ways to use locusts in her promotional efforts. She's looking into grasshopper bookmarks to supplement the ones she already has and she's not stopping there. "I'm collecting grasshopper items to display on my book table. I may even sell a line of inexpensive grasshopper products. I wear a grasshopper pin when I speak or call on stores. I had a baseball cap embroidered with a brown and green grasshopper, and I wear it with a more casual look. Anything to call attention to the book title, have people ask questions that lead me into describing the book."

Neither Nancy nor Jan spent a fortune, but they each generated a buzz about their books. There are a plethora of ideas out there, and you can take advantage of them. Are you a member of a critique group? How about having a brainstorming session to get ideas? Your family or coworkers might have lots of ideas if you ask them.

Advertising specialty professionals can not only help you think of intriguing ideas, they can also find items to fit your budget. Printed pens and t-shirts are just the beginning of what you can use to promote your book. Sheila Berndt of Commotion Promotions is one of the most creative and energetic people I know. Her article at the end of this chapter should get your creative juices flowing and help you understand more about advertising specialties.

Book Signings

Promotional items and advertising specialties can be used to drive traffic to your table during book signings. Depending on your book and budget, you can get real inventive during your signings.

Eva Marie Everson used something everyone enjoys when her book *True Love* (Promise Press) came out. "I gave away Hershey's Hugs and Kisses at my book table. When people walked up to me, I would say, 'Hello! Would you like a hug or a kiss?' Then I would tell them about the book." She did the same when the follow-up book, *One True Vow* (Promise Press) was released. She sold them together on the table, and the chocolate drew people in.

Don't have money to purchase giveaways? Your book is a great item to give to one special reader. Eva Marie wanted to increase her mailing list, as well as get people to her table, so she held a drawing. She used slips of paper, pens and a pretty crystal bowl on the table. She asked for names and addresses and, at the end of the signing, she drew a name. Winners do not need to be present to win as she mails the book to the winner after the event is over.

Book signings can be as painful as hitting your thumb with a nail, or they can be a party. It's up to you to arrange your signings and set the tone. You might have a difficult time getting your book carried in bookstores across the nation, but it's relatively easy to stage a signing close to home. A visit to the store owner, manager, or community relations person is all it takes.

Joanne Hill, author of *Rainbow Remedies for Life's Stormy Times* (Moorhill) found out how easy it is to schedule a book signing when she went to one at a Barnes and Noble store to see how the "big boys" did it. *Chicken Soup for the Traveler's Soul* was the featured book; but only Joanne, the author, and two employees showed up.

"I got into a conversation (raising my voice so people around could hear) with the author. This got a few more people to come and join in, as well as some hanging around the fringes. The next day the Barnes and Noble representative called, inviting me to come to their travel club to talk on my book."

Joanne says that idea had not crossed her mind. But after she spoke, the travel club sponsor picked up her book and read how travel had helped heal Joanne's grief. "We are all in this together," says Joanne. She learned the need to be receptive to new ideas and also about the importance of helping other authors. "I try to attend as many book signings as

I can at our local store. Barnes and Noble wants me back next fall to talk to the writers' club."

If you've created an excellent book with an engaging cover and a great title, bookstore managers are usually happy to have you in their store. For them it's a no cost, no risk way to hopefully increase sales and draw traffic into their store. You'll want to make sure they have ordered enough stock if a distributor carries your book. You can also bring your own books and sell them on consignment. Either way, always bring extra books in case you're successful beyond your wildest expectations.

The best time for a book signing is, of course, right after it is released. But that's not the only time to consider doing one. Two of Eva Marie's books are about wedding proposals and marriages that last. Valentine's Day and the traditional wedding month of June are two excellent selling opportunities on the calendar. Holidays are a natural time to sell books, but there are other times too. Several Web sites featured in the resource section of this chapter have an extensive list of holidays and designated days to consider when it comes to book sales.

I did a book signing at Barnes and Noble one year as part of their nationwide effort to promote writing for publication. The store held a series of workshops and featured books targeted to writers. Not only did *WriterSpeaker.com* sell out within an hour of my arrival, but the buyer also ordered the book for dozens of readers who wanted a copy.

Don't limit yourself to bookstores, however. Have you written the perfect wedding book? A bridal shop owner might jump at the chance to have an author as part of her promotional efforts. Does your novel have a character who loves to garden? Why not visit a florist or a nursery to ask the owner to not only sell copies of your book, but have you there for a special event. Any place where people gather, especially if that place is targeted to a hobby, geographic location, ethnic group, etc., should be considered as an outlet for your book. The worst people can say is no.

Don't rely on store personnel to promote your signing because they probably won't. Anything you can do to alert the media, prepare a poster, pass out flyers, or talk it up can only help.

When Eva Marie Everson and I released *Pinches of Salt, Prisms of Light* (Essence), we scheduled a Friday morning radio interview on the Christian station. We told stories and answered questions and told the listeners they could meet us the next day at one of three book signings scheduled at three different stores.

By the end of the last event, we were exhausted; but it was well worth it. Our signings were during the Christmas season; and on that particular day, the manager of the Christian bookstore said we outsold Max Lucado, James Dobson, Michael Card, and many other best-selling authors. People would come in and start their conversations with, "I heard you on the radio."

Anything you can do to promote your time at a store or other selling venue will help sales and hopefully get you an open invitation back. With your postcards, bookmarks, advertising specialties, and giveaways, you can turn an event into a happening.

Signings can be as casual as you at a table, or they can feature a talk or a class. I was in Memphis doing a Huntington's Disease speaking engagement and took the initiative to set up a signing at Davis-Kidd bookstore. Because my book is targeted toward people with a specific disease, it was likely that none of the customers had ever heard of the disease.

Instead of waiting for people to come by my table, I did a thirty-minute talk about the disease, telling inspirational stories from my book. A modest sized crowd sat in chairs provided by Davis-Kidd; and to my amazement, every book sold. Even more amazing was the fact that not one buyer had any connection with Huntington's. The stories I told had a universal appeal for those interested in Alzheimer's, Parkinson's, multiple sclerosis and other neurodegenerative conditions. Had people only seen the title, I probably wouldn't have sold even one book. Engaging my audience and meeting their needs helped sell books and educate people.

A friend of mine sent me an article about an author in San Francisco who had written a book aimed at cat lovers. She scheduled three hours for a reading and book signing but decided to make sure her signing was well attended. She convinced a representative of a pet food company to attend. She also got donations from local artisans and merchants including a homemade quilt, several pet-related gift certificates, and cat artwork. She encouraged visitors to enter a drawing for a dollar to win the donated prizes. The proceeds were donated to the SPCA and animal rescue.

Think of various tie-ins when you do a book signing or event. Asking companies and individuals to join in your marketing efforts makes great sense. Not only can they provide prizes, but they typically promote the event to their customers and encourage them to attend your event. If you have written a novel involving spouse abuse, for example, you can partner with a local women's shelter. For a book about cancer, you could approach a number of support groups, doctors, and pharmaceutical companies.

Whether you're targeting bookstores or other nontraditional retail outlets, you'll need to create a list of possibilities. Your local yellow pages are a good starting point; but the Internet is also a great help for searching out names, addresses, and phone numbers of stores you believe would be receptive to your book. Most chains have locator searches you can use to locate stores in your targeted area, complete with addresses and phone numbers. Yahoo.com offers a yellow-page search that allows you to look for businesses and nonprofit organizations by location and topic.

Once you locate target retail outlets that might be open to a book signing, call the store and ask to speak to the person who coordinates them. Sometimes it will be the manager, but often it's a community relations coordinator or publicity person. You can also stop in, though it's good to at least call and get the name and position of the correct person before arriving.

Once you reach the contact person, let them know you are an author interested in signing books. If your book is already in their distribution system, make sure to mention that. If your book is not in their system—and even if you are published by a royalty publisher there is no guarantee your book is in their database—you can always work on consignment or give them the information needed to order the book from your distributor. You'll find more information about distributors later in this book.

Make sure you have your calendar available because your goal is to get a date scheduled. You'll want to think about obvious tie-ins as you choose a date. They may need to get back to you or have you call at another time. Once you have a date, request the information they need for your event to be included on the store calendar that is posted for all to see, used as a flyer with every purchase, or sent to the local newspaper.

After a date has been chosen, offer to mail, e-mail, or drop off information about your book that the store can use for publicity. A copy of your book cover, your press photo, a brief author's bio, and reviews and blurbs are appropriate to send.

Call at least a week before your signing to confirm your books have arrived or are scheduled to arrive before the signing. Always throw a case of books into your trunk in the event your books don't arrive or if the store's stock sells out.

Ask the store contact person if someone will be creating a poster to be displayed a few days before and during your event. Be prepared to bring your own, featuring you and your book. Confirm that you can use the store's easel, or bring your own.

Always ask if your books can be displayed, not only at your table but at the register and, if appropriate, in an area reserved for local authors. Bring a friend with a camera to take pictures of you with customers and bookstore staff. These can be placed on your Web site and also sent to the media with a press release or article.

If there are any books left, offer to sign them. Customers love autographed copies even when they have not met the author. If you have foil "Autographed Copy" stickers, ask to have them affixed to the books you leave.

Larry James, author of *How to Really Love the One You're With: Affirmative Guidelines for a Healthy Love Relationship,* has compiled an outstanding list of ideas to make your book signing successful. Larry has over twenty other tips on his Web site in addition to the twenty he graciously allowed me to share with you at the end of this chapter. You don't have to use all of them at once, but hopefully you'll find ways to make book signings fun and profitable.

Featured Authors

Jan Coleman	www.jancoleman.com
Eva Marie Everson	www.evamarieeverson.com
Larry James	www.celebratelove.com
Nancy Lindquist	www.njlindquist.com
Wendy Lawton	www.wendylawton.com

Featured Resources

Advertising Specialties

Sheila Berndt	www.commotionpromotions.com

Holidays and Events

Celebrate Today	www.celebratetoday.com
Earth Calendar	www.EarthCalendar.net
FoodHealth.com	www.foodandhealth.com/calendar
The Daily Globe	www.dailyglobe.com/day2day.html
Web Holidays	www.web-holidays.com
Worldwide Holiday & Festival Site	www.holidayfestival.com

Print Promotional Items

Printing for Less	www.printingforless.com
NRS Publicity Printing	http://my.athenet.net/ ~nrsprntg/index.html

Postcards

1-800 POSTCARDS	www.1800postcards.com
Color Printing Central	www.colorprintingcentral.com
Modern Postcard	www.modernpostcard.com
Quality Printing Cheap	www.qualityprintingcheap.com/ postcard.html

Post Offices

United States	www.usps.com
Canada	www.canadapost.ca

Samples

www.writerspeaker.com/youcan.html

Cover Story

by Deborah Raney

With a bit of advance planning, the cover of your book can go to work for you long before the book hits the bookstores or the binding is even on the book.

As soon as your publisher has a cover design for your approval, request that they print 300-500 extra cover flats when they go to press. These overruns cost the publisher a pittance, but are worth their weight in gold when it comes to promoting your book.

Ask your publisher to ship the covers to you flat and trimmed, but in one piece. (If your cover will be embossed, request they not run these promotional sheets through the embosser.) Using a paper cutter or craft knife, cut each cover into three pieces—front cover, back cover, and spine. A professional printer can also cut these for you at minimal cost.

Here are some ways you can use each piece to allow your cover to pave the way for your book's upcoming release.

Front Cover

- To make an oversized postcard, run the front covers through an inkjet or laser printer, printing an intriguing "blurb" about your book on the back, lefthand side. Address the righthand side, stamp, and send these announcements to your mailing list of fans and readers.
- Print a short bio, a list of your books in print, and your Web site information on the back and use as giant business cards to hand out at book signings, speaking engagements, etc.
- At book signings you can autograph or personalize these cards for people who plan to buy your book when it comes

---

Deborah Raney is the author of several nonfiction books and five novels, including *After the Rains* (WaterBrook), the sequel to her highly acclaimed *Beneath a Southern Sky*. Deb's first book, *A Vow to Cherish* (Bethany), inspired a World Wide Pictures award-winning film of the same title. Visit her Web site at homepage.mac.com/debraney.

out. Readers can post this on their refrigerator or bulletin board to remind them to watch for your book's release.

- After your book comes out, it's nice to have these overrun covers on hand at book signings to autograph for shoppers who already own your book but forgot to bring it to the store with them, or who want to buy the book, but can't afford it until next payday.

Back Cover

- The back cover usually includes a short synopsis of the book, endorsements by other authors, and a photo of the author. Get permission to put a stack of these ready-made promo pieces on the desk at your local bookstores and libraries. It's a great take-home incentive to remind people to pick up your book the next time they are shopping or browsing the library. If you are available for speaking engagements, you can print your contact information on the back side.
- This also makes a perfect piece to include in the promotional packet you send to organizations where you will be speaking or signing books.

Spine

- The book's spine makes an excellent bookmark to give away at book signing parties, to make available to libraries and bookstores, or to hand out when you speak at an event.
- Depending on the layout and design of the spine, you may be able to cut it into traditional business card-size stock and print your contact information on the back. (Hint: It's easier to print this information before you cut the flats apart.)

Whole Uncut Flat Covers

- These are handy to have available to give to newspaper reporters, interviewers, or bookstore owners when you are promoting your book. Besides providing a convenient written synopsis of the book, I've found that many times, when I've made a cover flat available to them, newspapers and magazines will run a facsimile of my book's cover alongside my photo in the article.

With some creative inspiration, you can put your book's cover to work for you long before it serves its intended purpose—to cover the pages of your book.

Using Advertising Specialties to Sell Your Book

by Sheila Berndt

An advertising specialty is any item that can be imprinted, usually with a logo or catchy tag line. Advertising specialties are promotional handouts that can be the perfect tool to remind people to buy your book and tell others. A well-chosen item often remains on readers' desks, in their cars, in their pockets, or in their homes for a long time.

Advertising specialty experts should be passionate and creative. It is also their responsibility to guide clients to the best advertising specialty vehicle to carry their promotional message. When deciding the best item, budget, theme, demographics, and marketing goals all need to be considered.

The book marketplace is very competitive, and the covers of books are brighter and more intriguing than ever. A creative promotional handout specifically designed to fit your criteria will create additional excitement. It can make the difference from blending in with other books and authors to standing out head and shoulders above the crowd. An ad specialty will draw people to your book with its uniqueness, element of fun, and/or perfect match to your book's title or theme. It will make you and your book much more memorable.

There are infinite ideas for marketing your book using promotional items. The key is using an expert to guide you to items that will achieve the results you desire. There are terrific promotional items that are inexpensive, yet useful and powerful tools.

Sheila Berndt is an award-winning account executive with Commotion Promotions. She has been inspiring clients and helping them in their marketing efforts for over thirteen years. She loves turning creative ideas into creative items that accomplish her client's objectives. Visit her at www.commotionpromotions.com.

Readers love and use bookmarks, which don't need to be boring. They can have foam toppers, be created in custom shapes, be multicolored, or be memorable in some other way.

Magnets are a great vehicle and next to impossible to throw away; just look at your neighbor's refrigerator. They cost less than a postage stamp and are available in custom shapes, sizes, and colors. Post-it® notes are great because they travel. Custom imprinted notes come in endless shapes and colors (i.e., a foot-shaped sticky note for talking about the Christian walk), plus they get stuck to an array of papers that make the rounds to other people. Pens are a great giveaway at book signings and can be color coordinated with your book cover.

Here are some ideas and recommendations on how imprinted items can be used to support chapter titles, main title, or concepts:

- "Live for Today, Plan for Tomorrow": pocket calendar
- "Loving God with All Your Mind": stress squeezer that looks like a brain
- "Mending Your Heart": heart magnet, sewing kit, bandage dispenser with hearts imprinted on the bandages
- "Reshaping Your World": packets of clay
- "Nourish Your Soul": packets of cocoa, coffee, tea, or mixed nuts
- "Taking a Look at Ourselves": pocket mirror, bookmark magnifiers, computer mirror
- "The Ups and Downs of Life": yo-yo, Slinky® toy
- "Living the Word": lip balm (tag line: We give you more than lip service.)
- "Being a Good Steward of Time": magnet with clock imprinted on it, inexpensive timepiece
- "Sticking with Your Faith in Tough Times": Post-it® notes, magnet
- "Family": picture frame (can be magnetic)
- "Making Your Mark in the World": washable tattoos, markers, highlighters, flower seed packets
- "Light of The World": highlighters, flashlights
- "Brokenness": puzzle pieces, erasers

- "Getting a Grip on the Tough Times": jar grip opener
- "A Question of Rule": bookmark/rulers
- "Garbage In, Garbage Out": litter bags

Whatever the title or main idea of your book, there's a unique, promotional giveaway perfect for achieving your sales goals.

20 Ways to Make Your Next Book Signing an EVENT!

by Larry James

Here are some tips and suggestions that have helped me increase the number of books sold at a book signing. Many are my own, and some were suggested by other author friends. Each bookstore has its own distinctive personality. While I do not attempt to do all of the suggested tips at every signing, it is important to adapt as many as you can to fit each store's personality. Believe me, doing so will increase the opportunity to sell more books.

1. DO - Write your own announcement for the bookstore's intercom. Make it short and brief. Give the manager several versions because he usually announces that you are there several times. Don't hesitate to remind someone to make the announcement again if it's been awhile since the last one. Personnel often will get busy and forget. Every half hour should do it. If you do lectures or give speeches about your book and are in town for a keynote or seminar that is open to the public, include information about that too. Let the bookstore manager choose to include it in the announcement or not.

2. DON'T - Don't just sit at the table provided for you. Most authors do that. Be different! Reach out and touch someone! Don't wait for them to come to you. I always tell the person booking the signing not to worry about putting a chair behind the table. This

---

Larry James is a professional speaker and author of *How to Really Love the One You're With: Affirmative Guidelines for a Healthy Love Relationship, LoveNotes for Lovers: Words That Make Music for Two Hearts Dancing!* and *Red Hot LoveNotes for Lovers*. Visit his site at www.celebratelove.com. Adapted from Larry's "40+ Ways to Make Your Next Book Signing an EVENT!!" To read more great tips, visit www.celebratelove.com/booksigningtips.htm.

will always get her attention. Let her know you will be the store's official greeter while you are there. Walk around the store with several copies of your book and introduce yourself to everyone.

3. DO - Request at least a dozen books for your table to show you have plenty available. If those you introduce yourself to show the least bit of interest, hand them a book. They will almost always take it. Tell them to look at it and bring it back to the table when they are finished. On average, I more than tripled my book sales at signings by implementing this tip!

4. DO - Have an attractive, four-color bookmark designed by a graphic artist and print thousands of them. You can give them to everyone who comes in the store. List a few endorsements on it, as well as a brief paragraph of what the book is about. Leave your contact information off. Put the price and the ISBN on. Bookstores often have their own bookmarks, and staff members are reluctant to have you give yours out if they think their customers are going to you directly. (I use a red rubber stamp to imprint my Web site address on the reverse side of the bookmarks I give out in the store, but not on the bookmarks I leave at the store.)

I often will sign a bookmark for someone who lingers at my table but does not buy my book. Remember your mission: "Spread good will!" Many people will come back to the store and buy your book after you have left. Send the bookstore several hundred bookmarks, and suggest that staff members include them in the bags for people who buy books before your book signing.

5. DO - Send the person who booked the signing a brief thank-you note. I'm told that authors seldom do this. I've had several people call me to thank me for sending the note.

Write a follow-up commendation letter to the CRC's [community relations coordinator] manager as a fantastic way to thank and build good relations with both the CRC and the bookstore.

6. DO - Remember to call at least two months in advance if you want to be included in the in-store flyer.

7. DO - Go to Kinko's and have your book covers enlarged in color to an 11 x 17 poster, laminate them, and have them put on a poster-type board with a standup easel on the back. Always bring them with you to the signings. Anything else you can think of to call attention to your table is also *great!*

8. DO - Ask the CRC for a media list (radio, TV, etc.). Some don't have them, but the ones who do will usually share it or tell you where to get it. It makes calling the radio and TV stations easier. If they don't have a media list, ask them which stations they would recommend that might be interested in an interview. When they know you are also doing stuff to promote the signing, usually they do more too!

9. DO - Ask for a community list, i.e., Chamber of Commerce, Society of the Arts. Send them a news release about your book signing (and seminar or keynote, if applicable). You never know where your speaking engagements may come from. Check first with your meeting planner to get permission, then add a personal note to the news release inviting them to come and hear you speak. (You do accept speaking engagements to talk about your book topic, don't you?)

10. DO - Although most bookstores will send a news release about your book signing, send your own as well. This increases the chance of getting coverage. Send it at least two to three weeks in advance to all media within a fifty-mile radius. Include a photograph of yourself and a book cover. Tell all about your book; yourself; and, if you are doing a talk instead of just a book signing, include your topic title and a little bit about it. Include your phone number and the contact person, address, and phone number of the bookstore. Editors often will call you or the store for more information.

One more thing. Always confirm that the CRC will send a news release to the media. I no longer will do book signings at stores that are not willing to send news releases about my book signings.

11. DO - Put several of your books "face out" when staff members aren't looking! I often will also put the books of my author friends "face out."

12. DO - Send your endorsements. Print them in an attractive, large font on a white sheet of paper. CRCs will often use them on posters, etc. Also send several book "covers." Request that they put up a special display, including poster, at least a week in advance of the signing. Most do, but it doesn't hurt to ask.

13. DO - Ask the manager how many books he would like you to sign before you leave, so the store will have some on hand. Note: Generally speaking, stores cannot return any books you sign, so always ask! If the signing went well, or even if it didn't, and you impressed the manager, he will usually have you sign a bunch before you leave.

14. DO - Bring a camera and have your picture taken with the manager or CRC and other key people in the store. If you want to call attention to yourself, pay attention to other people. Most people don't do this. You may want to use several of the photos in publicity in the future.

To take this idea a step further, make sure your book is in the picture. Next, buy an inexpensive frame; and mail the photo in the frame, along with a handwritten, personal note, suggesting the CRC hang the picture in a conspicuous place in the store. You might also suggest that she start an Authors Photo Wall (or Hall) of Fame. The CRC will be more than happy to have her picture with you hanging in the store, and you and your book will get more frequent recognition.

15. DO - Have copies of readers' reviews available at your table. Hand them to anyone who shows the least bit of interest in your book and say, "Here's what other people who have read my books have to say." Make extra copies for giveaways. One of my books is called *LoveNotes for Lovers;* so I say, "Here are some LoveNotes from some of the people who have read my books." When someone begins to read the reviews, remain quiet. Amazon.com is a good source when people post impartial reviews of your book. Most people hold Amazon.com in high regard. If no reviews are posted, send the link to your book to your friends and encourage them to post reviews.

16. DON'T - Don't complain if you don't sell lots of books. You must realize that signings and book readings or presentations will rarely exceed your expectations and hardly ever meet your highest goals. Signings make those who bought your book feel good, but they generally don't sell lots of books while you are there *unless* you create a presence *while you are there.*

I've sold as few as none to as many as fifty-six books in a two-hour period. According to bookstore managers, on average, book sales for a noncelebrity author will range from four to seven. If you sell more, you're doing great!

17. DON'T - Don't show your disappointment if you don't sell very many books. It only creates bad will. Book signings and presentations will rarely exceed your expectations. The community relations coordinator will often be apologetic if the response wasn't good. This is your chance to thank her for the opportunity and ask for another book signing in the near future. Nuff said!

18. DO - Talk about other authors' books—authors you know. I have a story in *A 2nd Helping of Chicken Soup for the Soul* and always ask the manager to put those books on the table too. I sign on page 18 under my name. I know my friends Mark Victor Hansen and Jack Canfield, the "Chicken Soup" guys, don't need my help; but the customers love it! My dear friend, Greg Godek's book, *1001 Ways to Be Romantic* often shows up on my table. He mentions one of my books in several of his.

19. DO - Come bearing gifts! Give the community relations person (or the person who booked the signing) a rose, small bunch of flowers, or a tiny box of chocolates. That person will not forget *you!*

20. DO - MOST IMPORTANT: Have FUN! Let people know you are there to have fun, even if you don't sell any books. The manager of the store often feels worse than you do because he or she is afraid you won't come back. Have fun! Create attention!

Some final words: It is important for you to understand that the purpose of book signings is not necessarily to sell books, but to make the bookstore customers *aware* of your books.

Chapter

Caulking the Gaps
Media Promotions

Circumstances may cause interruptions and delays, but never lose sight of your goal. Prepare yourself in every way you can by increasing your knowledge and adding to your experience, so that you can make the most of opportunity when it occurs.

—Mario Andretti

In *Lilies of the Field,* Homer, a Baptist, talks to the village Catholic priest who has been holding church services outdoors in the back of a pie wagon. The priest is somewhat bitter because his dreams of greatness have seemingly not been answered.

"When I was ordained, how I prayed," the father said. "How I prayed for a call to a great, majestic cathedral in some wealthy diocese." For years he sent the call up in English and Latin, but he didn't like God's answer.

Maybe you've prayed about how to get your books into the hands of those you know God wants you to serve. God always answers prayers, but sometimes we don't like the answers. We want to hear, "Yes!" Instead we often hear, "No" or "Wait."

The priest thought God was saying, "No." In reality, for many years He was saying, "Wait." That became obvious when, because of a stubborn nun and a handyman, the church was finally completed. During his waiting time, God prepared the priest. Humility became part of his character, and that adobe church was a magnificent cathedral to the man who now simply wanted to serve God.

Do you feel as if God is saying, "No," when it comes to your media efforts? That feeling might be because you are trying to make things happen on your own and you have bought into the hype that only by being on Oprah can you sell books.

At church one Sunday a visiting pastor said something of great relevance to those of us who seek to spread the good news through our writing. He said, "The Lord of history makes the decisions, not Oprah." Of course I knew that, but hearing it helped me keep my focus as one who has not been on Oprah or any other national show that makes authors an "instant success."

As you enter the confusing world of newspapers, television, and radio, it's important to remember that promotion is a process that must be built on prayer. We need to pray with reverent confidence, and we must have a relationship with God. We must also be willing to know and follow the rules.

Do you start your media efforts locally, regionally, nationally, or internationally? In most cases beginning close to home has distinct advantages. Selling yourself in your own community is usually more comfortable for both the buyer and seller. There are no long distance phone bills and minimal travel costs. You often know people in your town who are interested in your work. Media outlets are more likely to feature local writers talking about local issues, or at least playing up the hometown angle. However, if you limit your marketing efforts to local venues, you probably won't sell as many books as you'd like. More importantly, the people who need to read your book won't know it exists.

Eventually you'll need to expand your market, and you might have to do a variety of different things. This book covers a huge array of marketing tools, some of which will work for you and others you might want to ignore. Some authors have titles that lend themselves well to national television, while others would be better served sticking to the local Christian radio station.

Whether you're pitching *Good Morning America, The 700 Club,* or your local NBC affiliate, it takes being a professional to get the desired results. Of course, bathing your efforts in prayer is essential, but there are other things to remember when it comes to dealing with the media.

Awareness

I'm constantly amazed at the number of authors who do not read newspapers, rarely watch the nightly news, and live in their own little worlds. Being aware of what is happening is key to working with the media to promote your book. Did a prominent member of your community embezzle from the area's largest firm? You can bet that if that happened, it would be the talk of the town for several days or weeks. If you've written a book on character, this would be the perfect time to contact reporters and producers for an interview. It's during times of crisis and conflict that people seek solutions, and maybe your book offers ways to build character in our children or even in ourselves.

Credibility

Being aware of news stories around the world gives you a calling card. It takes enormous effort to write and publish a book, and in most people's eyes your having authored one gives you instant credibility. Capitalize on that credibility and what's happening in the world to seek out media opportunities.

Learning to be a great guest with solid interview skills will boost your credibility like nothing else. Two articles at the end of this chapter offer helpful advice. Ellie Kay is a best-selling author, international speaker, and national radio commentator and regular on CNBC's number one rated *Power Lunch* program. She is also the author of *Heroes at Home: Help and Hope for America's Military Families.* (Bethany). Her article, "12 Strategies for Your On-Camera Interview," should help you as you prepare for your interviews.

Timing

We've all heard that timing is everything, which is especially true with the media. Back- to-school, holidays, elections, and anniversaries are all time sensitive. Tiny windows of opportunity allow you to promote your book, but you have to work on deadlines set by the media. Most magazines have already put their Christmas issues to bed in May, and guests for Mother's Day are often scheduled and filmed months in advance. Several Web sites at the end of this chapter list the obvious and not so obvious dates for events and celebrations that might be perfect for marketing your book. Always confirm the deadline for getting information to the producer or reporter.

Lisa Copen, of Rest Ministries, understands the benefit of marketing around designated days. She is a sponsor of National Invisible Chronic Illness Awareness Week in September. She recently sent out a press release to authors and owners of Web sites who might have a book targeted to those suffering from chronic fatigue syndrome and other related diseases. Lisa suggests using online chats to promote books, a topic I'll develop in a later chapter.

With her e-mail message, Lisa attached a short blurb, perfect for a newsletter, e-zine, etc., a longer press release, and facts about chronic illness. What a perfect way for authors to reach out to those with a specific need. She encourages authors with a book to schedule a time for an organized chat that will not only help those interested in this subject learn more, but hopefully sell books. This is only one of thousands of designated days, weeks, or months that authors can use as marketing tools.

Patience and Persistence

Wayne Dyer said, "Infinite patience brings immediate results," and that is certainly true when dealing with the media. Sometimes the timing is perfect, and everything falls into place. More often success doesn't happen instantly. Usually an idea needs to be planted and nurtured with a heavy dose of patience before we see results. Rejection is part of promotion, just as it is in publishing. You can't take either personally, and you simply have to be patient while you work at creating opportunities.

When a door opens, even a tiny crack, you'll need to somehow get inside. Thomas Edison said, "Everything comes to him who hustles while he waits." This perspective is a key to successful marketing.

Realistic Expectations

Face it. Most of us will never be on Oprah or CNN. This is just the way it is. Accepting reality in no way means you're a quitter, but it does free you up to do more and better interviews, write and publish more books, and build your credibility and stature.

One of the first rules of publishing is to know what the publisher wants and who reads their books. The same is true when it comes to the media. For example, if you have written a book about the dangers of sex outside of marriage, you'd be wasting your time pitching *Cosmopolitan,* for obvious reasons. This magazine and its readers don't accept the reality that abstinence is not only possible but an incredible blessing. There are many radio and television shows, both Christian and secular, that would love to have you as a guest, however, so focus on those instead of setting yourself up for failure.

Follow Up

Even a rejection is an opportunity for follow up. A thank-you note and a new spin on an idea three months later are ways to keep your name in a producer's or reporter's mind. Marketing is about relationships with both the buyer and those who can help you reach your target market. Of course, you'll want to follow up after each interview and when there's an obvious opening. After the local NBC affiliate did an interview with me, I sent the reporter a thank-you note. This fall I'm hosting our first conference for caregivers of those with Huntington's Disease. You can be sure I'll contact this same reporter to let her know about the conference and accompanying charity walk. I'll frame my information as newsworthy and hope for the best.

Books on Shelves

There's nothing worse than giving a magnificent interview that inspires people to run out and buy your book, only to discover it has to be special ordered. Most customers want the book now, and many aren't willing to wait days or weeks to get a book they heard about on the radio or television.

Brenda Nixon is proactive when it comes to getting the word out: "When I have a scheduled radio interview, I don't let it stop there. Before the interview, I contact libraries, bookstores, and churches in the area to alert them to the interview. Almost always the libraries and bookstores will order copies of my book. Then I make a deal with them. If they get copies of my book on their shelves before the radio interview, I'll tell listeners to get my book at those locations."

If your book is not readily available in bookstores, and even if it is, make sure you have several ordering options for potential buyers, such as your personal Web site, an online bookstore, and a fulfillment house with a toll-free number.

Ellie Kay sells books from her Web site, but she also is listed with Amazon.com. According to Ellie, the Amazon rankings are not an effective tool to measure the total number of books sold. She says it is, however, a good tool to use immediately following an interview to gauge the general effectiveness/viewership/listenership of that interview.

> Here is how it works. Make a note of your ranking before your radio or TV interview airs and then after to see if there is a "bump" in the Amazon.com rankings. For example, one of my books ranked around 90,000 before *Midday Connection* and then sold enough books to drop down to less than 1,000 by the end of the day. It leveled out at around 35,000 for the media campaign for that year. This tells me that people were listening, visiting the book's page at Amazon, and buying it.
>
> The same was true on my last book release this past spring. It was a new release in January. I went on CNBC's *Power Lunch* in February and the rankings jumped from 500,000 to 325 within five minutes of the show's international exposure.
>
> On the other hand, I was on a national nonreligious TV show called *Lifestyles Magazine* that was syndicated and had an episode air and re-air several times. Each day it aired, there was not a single bump on Amazon, which means hardly anyone who buys books watched this show and/or they didn't promote the book on the show very well! This helps us decide which radio/TV shows to fit into our schedule and which ones do not get the exposure that may warrant our time investment.

Ellie gives us a little more insight into what this might mean for an author:

> Keep in mind that your rankings can jump from 500,000 to 1,000 during a media campaign and still settle out at around 200,000 or more. But if your numbers are consistently 50,000 and below, then the Amazon indicators tell us that your books are fairly consistently selling in the nonreligious world, even if it's only a few books a day. What is amazing is that books by best-selling authors, such as Patsy Clairmont and Barbara Johnson, can sell 100,000+ books in the CBA marketplace and yet only hold a ranking of 180,000 at Amazon. So, as you can see, Amazon is not a definitive measurement of total book sales or the overall "success" of a book.

For a quick, easy tool to check the comprehensive Amazon.com rankings (and reviews) of all your books on one page, go to Amazon Lite at www.kokogiak.com/amazon.

Ellie has another way that Amazon.com has helped her in dealing with the media. In her experience in recent network media engagements, the overwhelming majority of nonreligious media producers will take a peek at Amazon.com before they even ask to see your media kit. They want to get a feel for what your book is about, check the success of the book, and get a feel for the feedback of the potential viewing/listening audience.

Ellie has specific suggestions about your Amazon page:

This is why the book description is so critical, as well as your book reviews that are posted there. If you have a fan write you about "how much they love your book" (or they approach you at a conference to tell you the same), then ask them to please write their comments at Amazon and Barnes and Noble.com.

Also, if you get a negative review that could really hurt your reputation/opportunity with these producers, then you can petition Amazon to remove the review if it does not fit their general criteria. For example, the reviews should never have been posted in the first place if (1) they attack the author personally rather than the work, (2) they are written with political/social/religious agenda in mind (i.e., Mormons bombarding an anti-Mormon book), and (3) they contain misinformation.

Working with the media can be intimidating. But once you get started, you'll probably enjoy it. Remember, each newspaper and magazine counts on authors to help fill some of the space not allocated to advertising. Television and radio shows need enthusiastic, interesting guests. The second article at the end of this chapter, *Toto and the Wizard of Oz: Demystifying the Author Interview* by Kyle Liedtke of MediaTalk, should make you more comfortable about interacting with media professionals.

Once you've landed an interview, be prepared with several colorful and dramatic sound bites. You should avoid jargon or unfamiliar words; and, if you must use them, provide quick explanations. It's normal to be nervous; and most people have a tendency to talk too fast, use incomplete sentences, or both. If you get a question you're not prepared for, repeat or rephrase it to give yourself a chance to come up with an answer. Remember that only you can talk about your subject and book in your unique way. Most of all, have fun.

Hopefully after reading chapter four, you feel comfortable creating media kits and press releases because those are key tools in reaching the media. Remember those rules I mentioned? Most interviews are given as a result of a media professional receiving a written pitch that piques someone's interest. At the end of this chapter, Kim Garrison of CLASS Promotional Services, shares her secrets in her article, "Writing an Interview Pitch That Gets You on the Air."

The following research section includes a variety of helpful Web sites for those who are interested in reaching various media. Take the time to investigate each site and learn how it can help you in your efforts to sell more books.

Featured Authors

Lisa Copen	www.restministries.org
Ellie Kay	www.elliekay.com

Featured Resources

Amazon.com Rankings

Amazon Lite	www.kokogiak.com/amazon

Holidays and Events

Celebrate Today	www.celebratetoday.com
Earth Calendar	www.EarthCalendar.net
Food and Health.com	www.foodandhealth.com/calendar
The Daily Globe	www.dailyglobe.com/day2day.html
Web-Holidays.com	www.web-holidays.com
Worldwide Holiday & Festival Site	www.holidayfestival.com

Media Consultants

B&B Media Group	www.tbbmedia.com
Kyle Liedtke	www.mediatalk.biz
Kim Garrison	www.CLASServices.com

Media Searches

Associated Press	www.ap.org
Christian Newspaper	www.christiannewsassoc.com/

Association   participate.html
Christian Radio.com   www.christianradio.com
Gebbie Press   www.gebbieinc.com
Network for Good   www.networkforgood.org/
                                                 speakout/index.html
News Directory   www.newsdirectory.com
NewsLink   www.newslink.org
NewspaperLinks.com   www.newspaperlinks.com/
                                                 home.cfm
Radio Locator   www.radio-locator.com
Reuters   www.reuters.com
United States Newspapers   www.50states.com/news

News Releases
Assist Ministries   www.assistnews.net
Christian Media List
   (fee service)   www.ChristianMedialist.com
DeMoss Newspond   www.demossnewspond.com
Internet for Christians   www.gospelcom.net/ifc
   newsletter
International Press   www.ipanews.com
   Association (fee)

Twelve Strategies for Your On-Camera Interview

by Ellie Kay

The first time I was on national television, I hugged a man wearing orange makeup, spun a money wheel, and ultimately walked away from the studio with $20,000 in merchandise. In case you haven't guessed, the name of that show was *The Price Is Right.* Even though I never imagined it at the time, this was to be the first of *hundreds* of national and local television appearances.

My debut interview on regional TV in New York went so well that the station offered me a regular job as the host of *The Savings Tip of the Week with Ellie Kay.* But on the first weekly show I did, I wore the wrong clothes and was cut off mid-sentence by the host, so they could go to the commercial break. In other words, I bombed. Big time.

The difference between these two successes and one failure lies in the area of preparation. Before I went to visit *The Price Is Right* studios, I did my homework and discovered they interviewed the whole studio audience to find potential contestants. By asking the right questions of people who had gone to the show, I found out the one basic question the producer asked: "What do you do for a living?" I rehearsed my response at home, trying to act extra energetic, and was well prepared when I got to the studio.

At the initial New York interview, I did the same thing. I practiced my short answers at home. But when I was on my first weekly show (where I bombed), I didn't rehearse the three-minute segment at home. Consequently, the live show went long. By the

---

Ellie Kay is a best-selling author, international speaker, national radio commentator, and regular on CNBC's number-one rated *Power Lunch* program. Her financial books have changed the lives of thousands of families, and her latest release is *Heroes At Home: Hope and Help for American Military Families* (Bethany). For information on Ellie's schedule and money-savings links, go to www.elliekay.com. Ellie's "Interview Preparation Worksheet" is available on my Web site at www.writerspeaker.com/youcan.html.

following week, I'd make the proper time modifications; practiced short answers at home; and, from then on, it was smooth sailing on the air.

Here are some tips to keep in mind when you go for a video or television interview, so it will succeed instead of bombing.

Prepare

Part of the preparation process is to take the time to think about your answers to any preinterview questions. Have a friend conduct a mock interview with you at home, and videotape it. Review the tape, looking for nervous mannerisms, distracting gestures, and your general appearance on camera. Experiment with different clothing to find the look that fits you best.

Confirm Your Appearance

Many studios will confirm your appearance the week of the event. If you do not get a call from a producer or assistant, then call the studio the day before the event and confirm the booking.

Dress Appropriately

Ask the producer ahead of time what style of clothing the on-camera talent wears. If the interviewer wears a suit, then so do you. If he or she is more casual, then dress the same. If you can view the show ahead of time, you'll have a better idea of what you should wear.

Never wear white, black, plaid, or hounds-tooth check as they don't work well on camera. At the very least, wear clothes that are dressy-casual. Remember that the camera adds ten pounds to your frame, so a long, lined sheath dress or a suit with matching jacket and pants will make you look thinner on camera. A contrasting, brightly colored shirt underneath the suit will make you look more energetic and alive on screen. If you're a woman, experiment with a printed scarf; but be sure you do a video camera check before you wear it on the set.

Be Well Groomed

You may be tempted to think that the lens doesn't pick up details on camera. But clothing stains, dirty hands and fingernails,

and unruly hair will be distracting on the air. Have a friend, production assistant, or the makeup person look you over critically
from head to toe before you go on. (Keep in mind that wide-angle
shots will pick up your full body length.) Ladies, if you wear nail
polish, make sure it's not chipped or peeling.

If the station does not have a makeup artist, then a good rule of
thumb is to wear the same amount of makeup you would wear if
you're on stage in front of a large audience, which is more than you
would wear normally. Now is the time to wear blush, eyeliner, and
mascara because your face can look washed out without extra color.

Maintain good posture, sit and stand up straight, and carry
yourself with confidence.

Come Alone

Come by yourself or with one friend who will not complicate
anything. You need to be able to focus on the task at hand without
the distraction of conversation with another person. I have trav-
eled with assistants who help with media and fully understand
what to expect once we get into the studio.

Be Punctual

Ask the producer to fax you a map, or go to
www.mapquest.com to find out how long it will take to get from
your hotel or house to the studio. Allow extra time for traffic and
getting lost. Arrive a little ahead of the time you're requested to be
in the studio (not more than fifteen minutes).

Know Names

Know the name of your interviewer, and confirm it on arrival
at the studio. Also know the name of the program and the time of
your on-air appearance. Print this information on the back of
your business card, and hand it to the receptionist. When you are
introduced to the interviewer, refer to him or her by title and
name, i.e., "Hello Dr. Hayter, it's so great to meet you."

Make a Good First Impression

The old saying, "You never get a second chance to make a first
impression," is especially true in television. Shake hands firmly,

and introduce yourself quickly and clearly. Walk confidently, and carry yourself well from the time you exit your vehicle until you enter it again to depart.

Be Courteous

Every studio, station, or show has different protocols regarding their guests. Be observant as you try to pick up on these courtesies. Wait until you are asked to be seated, be courteous and kind to everyone you meet, and sincerely compliment the show or an individual's work whenever possible. Before you go on camera, ask if it is all right to give out your Web site and contact information on the air.

Act Confidently

It is natural to be a little apprehensive before you go on camera. Even media veterans are concerned when they work because there's a lot riding on each show. It's important to remain focused before the cameras start rolling. Some effective ways to counter preproduction jitters are: (1) Be well prepared for the interview; (2) watch the show (if possible) ahead of time, so you are familiar with the set, format, and hosts; and (3) maintain good eye contact both on and off the set since it communicates confidence.

Clarify if Necessary

The time to ask for clarification about anything you don't understand is before the cameras start rolling. This is the time to ask how many segments will be involved in the taping and the length and emphasis of each segment. Ask questions about the audience in order for the best possible interview. For example, if you have a largely female audience or senior citizens, then you would adjust your answers to meet their specific needs.

Show Professionalism

Even if you don't have a vast amount of experience on camera, you can come across as professional by being positive, confident, and gracious. Pretend you are explaining your answers to your mother or father (someone who accepts you and loves you unconditionally), and don't try to put on airs.

A professional remembers two things:

- The other half of the communications equation is listening. You need to listen carefully to what the interviewer is asking you. The most important thing you can do is remember to think during your interview. How you speak and listen is critical in making a good impression.
- If you look the interviewer in the eye and smile, the camera will take care of itself. Answers should be comfortably brief, a couple of sentences at most. Remember to smile a natural, soft smile throughout your interview. Nod when the interviewer says something, and follow along carefully as he or she speaks to the viewers.

Don't Apologize

Never apologize for who you are, what you've written, or any lack of experience. If you make an error on camera, correct yourself if it's appropriate and quickly move on. Oftentimes the audience (and even the host) will not notice your blunder unless you point it out to them—and you *never* want to do that.

Toto and the Wizard of Oz: Demystifying the Author Interview

by Kyle Liedtke, MediaTalk.

To most authors, an interview is like going to the land of Oz; and the talk-show host is that great, green, bodiless, floating head of the Wizard who speaks with smoke, thunder, and lightning. The author sits shaking in front of the microphone, clicking her heels frantically, terrified that at any moment flying monkeys will swoop down and carry her off. The whole thing is dreadful.

That is, until Toto draws back the curtain.

Consider me your personal Toto (though I'm not nearly as furry). Let me draw the curtain on the wizard and demystify the interviewing process, so you can go home safely. But before you can go back to Kansas, you need to learn something about the wizard and something about yourself.

The wizard is powerful, but he's only a man pushing buttons. The wizard is only as powerful as the audience. Because of that, he or she will do anything the audience wants. So if you've been asked to be on a show, it's because the host or producer thinks you have something that will make the audience happy. If they don't have a happy audience, they don't have happy advertisers. If they don't have happy advertisers, the show is over.

Change your paradigm. You're not there for the host; you're there for the audience. Speak to them. Connect with them. Have something to say to them.

It's not all about you either, Dorothy. Dorothy was loved because she helped everyone else first. When you're in front of the

Kyle Liedtke is President of MediaTalk Communications. The passion of MediaTalk is to empower and equip messengers of God for the media. As a former talk show host, Kyle teaches how to communicate your message clearly and powerfully to and through the media and to excel during the pressures of live air time. His proven techniques have enabled authors, artists, spokespersons, and people everywhere to conduct themselves with confidence and passion in the media. MediaTalk. Learn the Language. For more information log onto www.mediatalk.biz, or call 541-390-9594.

microphone, don't sell your book. Find a heart for the tin man, find a brain for the scarecrow, give courage to the cowardly lion. This is what will endear you to the hearts of your audience. When a listener loves your book, she'll buy one. When a listener loves you, he'll buy all your books.

So follow the yellow brick road to good interviews.

Preinterview

Have Something to Say

The average attention span of a radio listener is forty seconds. Your answers should be no longer. Have a plan and purpose for your interview, arrange a theme statement and three to five key points, and then practice.

Get the Facts

Before the interview, get as much information as possible. Get the name of the host and program, style of program, and listener demographics. Get answers to these questions: How long is the show? Is it live or taped, and will there be time to edit? What is the purpose of the interview (the angle of the program)?

Confirm Your Booking

Confirm the specifics of the show, date, time, and length twenty-four to twenty-eight hours beforehand. Ask the producer if he needs anything like giveaways, extra press kits, etc. Request a tape of the program.

Always Be Early

If you are scheduled for a 1:30 live interview, be in the studio by 1:00. If the interview is live by phone, call in at least ten minutes before. (The producer may ask you to call back, but always be early.) If the interview is taped by phone, call at the time scheduled; do not call early.

Don't Expect a Second Chance

First impressions begin with the first person you come across in the parking lot of the studio or the first person who answers the phone. One of the biggest complaints about authors is that they're arrogant and rude. Unless you're Michael Crichton, you're not going to get away with it. Remember, we should have the attitude of Christ. I have interviewed hundreds of both secular and Christian authors and artists, and there is often little difference. In fact, most secular guests are more kind because they realize the direct relation between impressions and the advancement of their careers.

Always Bring Notes

Even professionals have off days when, for whatever reason, they can hardly remember the titles of their books, let alone remember the key points. Your notes should be on 3" x 5" cards only, never on paper. The microphone will pick up the sound of shuffling papers; and this will not only distract the listener, it will also send a subtle message that you're not fully ingrained with your material. Your notes should only contain key points and important quotes or excerpts from the book (which shouldn't be longer than a few sentences). But a word of caution here: If you're going to read excerpts or quotes from your book, be familiar enough with them that you can read them with inflection and emotion. I've literally had guests read their answers to me. (And I could hear the sound of thousands of people switching to another radio station!)

You should also bring blank 3" x 5" cards and a pen. You will use these cards to write the name of the interviewer and program name and/or station call letters on, then keep in front of you at all times. There is nothing that will break the connection of trust and credibility with the host and his listeners faster than if you say his name wrong. (Have you ever been to a concert where the artist says, "It's great to be in California!" when in Oregon? Notice how the crowd reacts and how long it takes for them to get back into the concert.)

Don't Drink Coffee Before or During the Interview

If you are offered something to drink, ask for a cold glass of water. (There is some evidence that drinking cold water helps the thinking process.) Any beverage with caffeine (coffee, tea, soda, etc.) will dehydrate you—especially your throat and mouth—making it difficult to speak for a long period of time. Caffeine is also a diuretic that will make you have to use the rest room often. The combination of these effects will only exaggerate any nervousness you might have.

Bring Breath Mints

Always, and I do mean *always,* have breath mints with you. Buy Altoids in bulk and keep tins everywhere—in your purse, briefcase, shoulder bag, coat pocket, desk drawer, car glove compartment—everywhere.

Forget Perfume

Avoid using much cologne or perfume; it can be distracting and overpowering in a small studio. There is also a chance that the people you come in contact with are allergic to perfumes.

Phone Interview Etiquette

Always offer to call the show. Remember you're not doing the host a favor, she is doing you one. So spend a few dollars.

First Impressions

When the receptionist answers the phone, clearly and cheerfully greet her, then identify yourself and request the producer and/or host of the program.

When the producer or host answers, be polite, but avoid chitchat. First thank him for allowing you on his show, then offer to give a "level" (that is, a test of your phone line and voice volume, i.e., "testing, 1, 2, 3, testing"). The quality of phones and phone lines vary so much that it is important for you to speak loudly and clearly. If your phone has a volume adjustment, set it on high. *Never* use a headset, cordless phone, or cell phone for an interview; the quality is often lower, and the risk of disruption is high. You want your message heard.

In-Studio Etiquette

Familiarize yourself with the studio and the station. Always ask where the rest rooms are and if there is a drinking fountain (if no one has offered you water). Better yet, always keep bottled water with you.

Let the Host and Producer Do Their Jobs

Be friendly, but don't initiate off-air conversation unless the host and producer appear to be available for it. If they are, ask questions about themselves: how long they've been doing the show, how long they've been in radio, where they're from, where they went to school, etc. Doing so will create a personable and positive atmosphere for the upcoming interview.

If the interview is live, ask when the commercial breaks are and if there would be time to use the rest room if you have to. (This will help you be prepared mentally in case you suddenly need to use the rest room in the middle of the interview.)

Ask about the Equipment

Every studio setup is different. Some interviewers will offer you headphones during the interview. If you're not familiar with using them, it can be disorienting. I recommend practicing with headphones at home and using them whenever offered. Ask how to adjust the volume, so it's barely above your speaking voice. Most studios have a "cough" button to allow you to turn off your microphone for a moment to cough, sneeze, or clear your throat. Ask if they have one. If not, just turn your head away from the microphone as far as possible and cover your mouth.

Every Microphone Is Different

Ask the host how close he would like you to the microphone and where he would like you to speak into it. Never be afraid to ask about the equipment. No radio guy expects you to be technically proficient. It is much better to be a novice than someone who acts like she knows what she's doing.

Interview

Show time. When the on-air light goes on, relax. You've done all of your preparation; and now it's time for you to take a deep breath, say a quick prayer, drink some cold water, clear your throat, and talk with the host. Keep eye contact with the interviewer, and talk to her like you're having a conversation over coffee. Be prepared, but be relaxed.

At the end of the interview, be sure to let your listeners know how they can get more information about you and your book. If you don't have a Web site, get one; it is the easiest way for people to pursue more information about you. Meanwhile, if you don't have a Web site and are listed on Amazon.com, tell people they can get more information about your book there. Make sure the host has this information as well.

Post-Interview

The first thing you should do after you've finished an interview is to write thank-you notes to the host and producer. Most talk show hosts keep a Rolodex™ of favorite and informative guests; get on the list.

The next thing you should do is to listen to your interview. Nothing will help you like hearing yourself. We all speak with words and phrases (and *uhs* and *ums*) that we don't know we're using until we hear ourselves. Practice.

Click, Click, Click

You're back home in Kansas, safe and sound. Yes, the great wizard was really only a little techno nerd. Nothing to be afraid of (except those flying monkeys).

Writing an Interview Pitch That Gets You on the Air

by Kim Garrison

Your book has just been released! Congratulations. Now a whole new phase begins: promoting your book, so everyone who needs your message finds out about it one way or another. Promotion in the form of radio and TV interviews should be part of your plan, so you will want to prepare a written pitch that convinces talk-show producers that they must invite you to be on their shows. Based on nearly two decades of experience promoting over a thousand authors to Christian broadcast media, following are some pointers from CLASS on crafting an interview pitch that gets you on the air.

General Information to Keep in Mind

Put yourself in the shoes of the talk-show producer (who is sometimes the host too). The main thing on his or her mind when considering your interview is, "Will this make a good radio discussion? Will the audience actually care about this?" So think about how to make your topic relate to the real-life needs of the listening audience, and don't just write about why your book is so great.

Also think about how you can make the talk-show host look good if he does this interview with you. In the vast majority of cases, the host will not have read your book, so he is relying on your written promo materials to conduct an intelligent, smooth-flowing interview.

Kim Garrison is the owner of CLASS Promotional Services, LLC, an independent division of CLASServices, Inc. After earning a B.A. in communications, she worked in Christian radio for five years and was later employed by the Dale Carnegie organization in San Diego. Since 1993, Kim has worked with Marita Littauer and CLASS and was trained by Marita herself in how to promote Christian authors and speakers. Today Kim runs one of the few publicity companies specializing in promotions for the Christian marketplace. You may contact her at 760-630-2677 or Kim@CLASServices.com. Visit CLASS at www.classervices.com.

Next, when writing your pitch, focus on the issue(s) you can discuss, more than the book. Link the book back to the issue. The live interview should lead to giving examples and content from the book that relate to the issue.

As for the writing style of the pitch, keep it straightforward, not flowery. What you write should explain simply and concisely why you and your book's topic will be an excellent choice for an interview. Another stylistic tip is to refer to yourself in the third person, as if someone other than you is writing about you.

Getting Ready to Write Your Pitch

Why did you write this book? What is your passion on this subject? Producers want to be able to sense what excites you about this content because that will translate into an exciting interview. Also, what is different about this book compared to similar ones? To answer this question, don't rely on the original research you did before writing the book. Investigate what has come out since then, especially the most recent releases. You must communicate what is unique and distinctive about what you have to offer as an interview guest.

Also think through how you hope this book will impact the lives of readers. Try to be specific in verbalizing the benefits you envision for people. Write them down. Then, with these in mind, identify the one specific thing you want to be sure to say during every interview. Some interviews are brief, and you may essentially only be able to make one point. For longer interviews, you'll want to know several other key points, so record those, too, as you prepare to write your interview pitch.

Components of Your Written Pitch

The following items are essential to include in the materials you compose to pitch your interview to a talk show:

- Book title and subtitle
- Author name
- Publisher
- Retail price of book
- Book summary

- Special features of the book
- Purchasing information
- Suggested interview questions
- About the author
- Author Web site
- Author availability
- Notes
- Interview contact information

Book Summary

This is the sales pitch to the talk-show producer and maybe the listeners, since it may get read on air as a promo for the interview. The copy should reflect what the interview is going to be on, rather than what the book is about. You could choose to concentrate interviews on only one part of your book—perhaps the most controversial or helpful part. If you're pitching the whole book, don't just duplicate the back-cover copy, especially if you're sending the book with the promo material.

Here are some tips for an effective book summary:

- Keep it brief. Two paragraphs should be plenty. Read the opening paragraph out loud and time it to be about thirty seconds. This will make it easy for the host to read as promo or intro copy for the interview.
- Make it personal. Write in the second person, such as in these opening lines from an interview pitch we once did: "Are you, or someone you know, part of a stepfamily? Do the issues you face as a stepparent seem overwhelming?"
- Aim to grab the attention of the producer. Is there a hot news story happening that links to your topic in some way? Feel free to mention that, but only as long as it's truly current news.
- Think about how to engage the emotions of the listener. For example: "How does one cope with the intense sorrow of losing a beloved spouse to death? What do you do when you feel as if your broken heart will never heal?"
- The opening paragraph should focus on getting attention, establishing the need, and introducing the issue. For

example: "Being a single mother is a challenging task, to say the least. Whether she's separated, divorced, widowed, or never married, a single mom may often feel overwhelmed with the responsibility of 'going it alone.'"

- Don't mention the book title or your name until the beginning of the second paragraph.
- Within the second paragraph, include a single biographical sentence to establish your credibility on this subject. You'll give more detail in a separate section later.
- Mention the title of your book a couple times in the second paragraph, perhaps setting it off in italic bold.
- Make your pitch personally relevant to the radio listener. What is he or she going to learn by listening to the interview?
- Try to end the pitch with a hope-filled, positive aspect of the proposed interview: "With the help of *Family Devotional Builder*, your whole family can enjoy fun and meaningful devotional times together."

Special Features of the Book

This section should be a handful of bullet points that highlight what stands out about your book. This is where you can focus more on the book itself than you did in the summary. Here are the special features from the pitch for one of Florence Littauer's books:

- Personality profile test identifies reader's personality type.
- Explanations and examples clarify the trademark characteristics of each personality type.
- Humorous anecdotes keep a lighthearted tone as readers identify problems.
- Concrete suggestions demonstrate how to resolve hot conflicts between spouses.
- Appendices: Timeline of Personality Discoveries, Overview of the Personalities, Personality Profile with Scoring Sheet

Purchasing Information

Tell how listeners can obtain a copy of your book. Christian bookstores? General bookstores? Internet? Which sites? Toll-free number? All of the above?

Suggested Interview Questions

Since most talk-show hosts won't have read your book, you can guide the interview by writing suggested questions, following these guidelines.

- Aim for about ten questions, some multipart. Avoid yes or no questions.
- Utilize a logical order in the questions, i.e., general to specific, chronological, or following your table of contents.
- Include page numbers where an interviewer can find the answers in your book when there is a direct correlation. Use this format after a question: (p. 35) or (pp. 35-40).
- The opening question should deal with background, i.e. "Why did you write this book?" (Phrase this question more creatively than that. For example: "When did you first get the idea to write this book? Who is the intended audience?") You may also suggest a question that asks how your book is unique compared to others that may seem similar.
- Think of questions that create a need for the book, so the listener has to go right out and buy a copy.
- Ask questions that allow you to give examples and illustrations from the book. You want to be able to tell stories as answers to some questions.
- If possible, try to include a question that would need a response about the book being given as a gift.
- The last question should offer hope. For instance: "What word of encouragement would you like to give today to a struggling single mom?"

About the Author

This section is a brief, but informative, bio about you. Mention your credentials, affiliations, education, accomplishments, and previous books published, if any. If you've contributed to major magazines, list those too. Also give personal information, including spouse's name, number of children, and where you live. Some producers will want to know about your local church involvement. If your name is unusual at all, spell it out phonetically, perhaps at the beginning of your bio, and make it bold. For instance, "Richard Abanes (pronounced **uh-BAH-niss**) has authored and co-authored over a dozen books on cults, the occult, and world religions."

Author Web Site

If you don't have a Web site, you should seriously considering setting one up. Today it is almost essential. Give the Web site address accurately. If it is something people frequently misspell, obtain both the correct and misspelled domain names. CLASS's Web site is www.classervices.com, but during an interview it is awkward to have to emphasize "only two ss" in the middle. Therefore, we now also own www.classservices.com (three ss).

Author Availability

Tell when you are available for interviews. The more flexible you are, the better. But be honest if you have certain scheduling restrictions (e.g., you are never available Monday mornings). Mention calendar blocks when you are unavailable (due to overseas travel, for instance), looking ahead three or four months. Don't ignore weekends; there are some talk shows that air live on Saturdays and Sundays. If you are pitching in-studio interviews, give dates and cities of your travel itinerary.

Notes

Here at CLASS, we label this section "CLASS Notes"; but you might want to call it "Of Special Interest" or just "Notes." This is where you can point out a certain holiday or other calendar event that will tie in nicely with your interview. Or you can tout the personality of the potential interview guest (you), your media experience, or anything else you want to convey that doesn't fit in the other sections. If you have a quote from a previous interviewer, this would be a good place for it.

Formatting Your Pitch Materials

There is no single best way to format your interview pitch materials. I've seen many formats that work nicely. Just keep in mind that you want to make the producer's job of evaluating your interview suggestion as easy as possible. She might spend only a few seconds scanning this page before deciding whether to pursue an interview or not! These tips should apply whether you design a printed sheet, an e-mail message, or a Web page that will be seen by producers:

- Keep your pitch concise. Don't get too wordy. One page (may be front and back if printed) for the whole thing is ideal.
- Use plenty of white space.
- Make it easy to follow with headings for all the sections, as mentioned above.
- Emphasize the contact information by placing it in a box or otherwise making it stand out.
- If your pitch page is primarily going to be faxed, use a sans serif font, such as arial.
- If this pitch goes out alone—that is, without the book— include a graphic of the book's cover somewhere on the page. A picture of you is nice too. If the pitch page is enclosed with the book, these graphics are less important.

I trust you now feel better equipped to compose an interview pitch that maximizes your chances to get on the air. And I hope that many talk-show audience members will be blessed by your interviews.

Chapter

Climbing the Scaffold
Developing a Speaking Platform

Let us not be content to wait and see what will

happen, but give us the determination to make

the right things happen.

—Peter Marshall

T hanks to Steven Spielberg's *Prince of Egypt,* even non-Christians are familiar with the life of Moses. In Exodus, God told Moses that He had seen the misery of His people in Egypt. He had heard them crying out and was concerned for them. That same God has heard the cries of those who read your books.

Each of you has a passion to write in such a way that you will be able to free people from depression, lack of forgiveness, anger, and other harmful emotions. Just as he rescued His people from the Egyptians, God wants to rescue all His children from the myriad of circumstances causing them pain. And just as God sent Moses to tell Pharaoh to let His people go, with your book He is sending you as a literature missionary. He might also be sending you as a speaker.

You all know the story. Moses wondered what would happen if Pharaoh didn't believe him. God gave him signs to prove that he had truly been sent from Him. Still, Moses had doubts about his abilities as shown in Exodus 4:10, "O Lord, I have never been eloquent, neither in the past nor since you have spoken to your servant. I am slow of speech and tongue."

Some of you have had that same argument when it comes to a speaking ministry. God's answer to Moses in Exodus 4:11-12 might apply to you: "Who gave man his mouth? Who makes him deaf or mute? … Is it not I, the LORD? Now go; I will help you speak and will teach you what to say."

If God is speaking to you about developing a speaking ministry, then rest assured He will be with you every step of the way. The good news is that even if you don't have a brother like Aaron who can act as your mouthpiece, there is training available to help you learn how to be an effective speaker.

If done well, speaking gives credibility to you as a communicator and can be a great way to sell your books. Not everyone is called to be a speaker, but training can help you understand if this is how you are called to communicate. Both Speak Up Speaker Services and Christian Leaders, Authors & Speakers Services (CLASS) offer excellent training programs for beginning and advanced speakers. From learning how to craft and deliver a speech to getting a better understanding of speaking as a profession, both of these organizations play a vital role in producing speakers who can go into all the world with God's message.

If you aren't a born speaker and if after intensive training you're still not comfortable standing behind the podium, don't despair. There are lots of other ways to sell books. But what if you do think speaking might be for you?

Years ago, on her first live album, singer Sandi Patty shared about her process of accepting who she was vocally. Sandi told how in high school she wanted to be Karen Carpenter, followed by wanting to be Barbra Streisand. As she became more polished she wanted to sing in an operatic style. Eventually she realized that she had been given her own voice and personality and she could be, not Karen or Barbra, but herself.

That's how it is with writing and speaking. There are probably many writers and speakers you admire, but God made you the way you are. You'll need to develop your own style and simply be yourself.

Want to know a secret? You've already read the back of the Book, and you know the end of the story. We win! Be bold as you proclaim the truth and share the good news. Training will help, as will practice; but mainly you need to be confident of your own abilities.

What else makes a good speaker? Knowing your subject matter, engaging your audience, using humor, being positive and challenging the audience are all ways to be an effective speaker. One resource for improving your speaking skills is *Dedicated Author*, a free e-zine edited by Sheila Seifert. Each issue features excellent tips for both writers and speakers. Subscription instructions are featured at the end of this chapter.

Most of all, you need practice to become the best possible speaker. You might consider joining your local Toastmasters group. This affordable organization provides training and competition on local, national, and international levels.

Most speakers tend to have a nonfiction book focused on a specific topic, but that doesn't mean speaking can't be as effective for fiction authors. Kristy Dykes is the author of 600 published articles and is now writing Christian fiction. Her first book, *American Dream* (Barbour), sold nearly 4,000 copies in ten months. She gives much of the credit for those sales to her speaking ministry: "My husband and I travel and speak across the Southeast and Caribbean. In our speaking engagements, I challenge people to strive for their dreams after telling them my dream was to see my Christian fiction published after all those articles. I give biblical tips for achieving a dream, which I define as 'a God-ordained desire'; and afterward, my book sells like hotcakes."

When *American Dream* hit the CBA best-seller list in July 2000 Kristy could barely contain herself: "I had to wipe a tear of joy away when I saw my name listed just a few slots below Jerry Jenkins and Tim LaHaye!" Her new book, *Sweet Liberty*, went into a second printing only weeks after being released.

Like many speakers, Kristy gets most of her speaking engagements through word of mouth. "My husband and I have been doing this for so long, we are known in our circles. He and I co-hosted our own TV show for five years, we've been guests on TV shows, and we hope to do more." She also has had her own radio show and done newsletter-type direct mail. Speaking is only one part of Kristy's marketing, but it accounts for a major portion of her book sales.

The same is true for Laura Sabin Riley, author of *All Mothers Are Working Mothers* (Christian Publications). When Laura has a speaking engagement, she finds someone who has been notably impacted by one of her books. "I simply listen as women talk with me beforehand and pay attention specifically when they graciously compliment my book and tell me why and how it has meant so much to them. I then ask one of these women (whoever did the most dynamic job selling my own book to me!) if she would say a few words to the others in attendance about how my book has impacted her."

According to Laura, when the ladies hear from one of their own, her books always sell to 30-50 percent of the audience. Since the industry standard is 10 percent this is a huge increase in sales.

Have you ever been sold on an upcoming movie after seeing the trailer? Isn't it disappointing when you discover that all the good parts were in the trailer and the rest of the movie wasn't worth seeing? That's how some speakers are with their books. Their speeches are only what's in the book. So either there's no reason to buy the book; or, when people do buy it, they are disappointed.

If you do decide that a speaking ministry makes sense for you, then make sure your speaking is not just a venue for book sales because your audience can tell the difference. Nothing is worse that a speaker behind the podium waving her book and screaming, "Buy my book!" at every turn. Your book gives your audience a reason to assume you are a credible source before you ever open your mouth; but your speech needs to be more than a sales pitch. Give your audience something beyond the content; but tie it back to the book, so they need to read what you've written to get the complete picture.

Increasing Book Sales

Once you're booked for an engagement, there are ways you can increase attendance. Depending on your topic or book, media outlets, such as local newspapers and talk radio, might be interested in your views. Take the time to craft a press release that outlines your key points from the book as well as your credentials. Remember those possible interview questions from chapter four? Here's a use for them. Contacting area bookstores makes sense if you have available time before or after your engagement.

One way to ensure book sales is to suggest that every member of the audience receive a book as part of registration. I recently provided the keynote message at an Alzheimer's conference. *Portraits of Huntington's* is obviously aimed at those dealing with Huntington's Disease. However, the subtitle, *Choosing Joy Through Life Lessons*, is applicable for everyone. The conference fee was initially $35 per person. I suggested the sponsoring organization buy 200 copies, one for everyone in attendance, at the wholesale cost of $10 each. The planners upped the fee to $45, and everyone got a copy of the book. By doing this, I was guaranteed $2,000 on top of my speaker's fee; and I shipped exactly what was needed early enough for them to add the books to registration packets. At conferences that have outside sponsors, such as pharmaceutical companies or other businesses, I suggest that the organizer ask them to underwrite the books given to those attending.

Another way I've worked with associations and groups has been to offer to donate a portion of all book sales from the event back to the organization. The donation can be used as a fundraiser, for scholarships, or any other purpose they desire. I have the organizer announce the donation when they mention the book's availability, and there's always an increase in sales.

Another great way to generate publicity and book sales is writing articles. That's true after the event, as well as before. Last year I spoke at the Huntington's Disease conference in Dublin, Ireland. After I got home, I offered to write an article about my time in Ireland. The article was printed in the sponsor's newsletter, along with my bio directing people to my Web site or Amazon.com. Several books have sold as a result of that article.

These are only a few ideas that could increase your book sales before, during, or after a speaking engagement. Professional speakers might want to join the National Speakers Bureau and exchange even more ideas.

Most speakers start small and speak on their books' topics. Church women's retreats, local charities or United Way, libraries, schools or other volunteer organizations are great places to start speaking. At some point, you will have enough practice to get a good speaking tape. Plus you'll want to invest in photos, an information sheet, and a Web site about you and your ministry, so you can expand your speaking ministry. At the end of this chapter, Marita Littauer's article, "Speaking to Promote Your Book," gives additional ideas on how to start your speaking ministry.

After completing the CLASS training, I began to count the cost of being a speaker. One of the first needs I had was for clothing. I had been a full-time caregiver for many years and had lived in shorts and casual dresses. While I might not wear power suits and heels like many speakers, I knew I needed to invest in several professional outfits. I also knew I had no extra money to spend.

I remember saying, "God, if you want me to be a speaker, please remember I have nothing to wear." That's it. I didn't make a big deal about my need to God, nor did I tell anyone about my pitiful wardrobe.

Soon after returning home, I got a call from Carol Kane, the owner of a furniture bank called Mustard Seed. When we moved to Orlando, we had to start over since moving furniture from Hawaii to Florida wasn't possible. Because my husband was ill, the furniture bank blessed us with a complete household of furniture. As my way of saying thank you, I began speaking for Mustard Seed through the United Way and other venues. Little did I know God was already training me to speak professionally.

A local designer outlet had donated 750 pieces of clothing to the Mustard Seed to be given away to women in need. Carol called to see if I'd like a new outfit. All I had to do was to go to the shop and have a local television reporter and photographer follow me around as I tried on various outfits. I said yes, so I could get a new dress but God had other ideas.

My first book had just come out; so before I began shopping, the reporter from a twenty-four hour news station interviewed me. What was supposed to be a brief bit of air time turned into a fifteen-minute segment. I was able to talk about Huntington's Disease; show the book cover; give my Web site and 800 number; and, more importantly, share my faith. That segment aired at least six times in a twenty-four hour period and was seen by thousands.

Following the interview, I was assigned a personal shopper and had fun trying on clothes. After a couple of hours, I had eliminated many dresses, slacks, and blouses; but I was having trouble narrowing my search to only one outfit. As the camera ran, I tried first one and then another for the store owner and personal shopper.

"Take them all," urged the owner. I'm not often speechless, but I certainly was after that generous offer. He was so moved by my story that he eventually gave me over $2,500 of designer clothes!

At one point in *Lilies of the Field,* Homer and Mother Superior discuss Homer getting paid for a job. Mother Superior quickly points to Matthew 6:28-29, "And why do you worry about clothes? See how the lilies of the field grow. They do not labor or spin. Yet I tell you that not even Solomon in all his splendor was dressed like one of these." Each time I wear one of my gorgeous outfits from that incredible shopping spree, I am reminded of these verses. God has an uncanny way of providing for us when we are in His will and doing what He calls us to do. Your need might not be clothing; but if God calls you to speak as a way to promote your book, He will also provide the training and opportunities.

One of the most frequently asked questions about speaking is how much to charge. While we all write to share a message, most of us would like to earn something for our efforts. Speaker's fees are often how authors afford to keep writing, so this is an important question.

God wants us to trust Him, and He also gave us discernment to know when speaking for free makes sense and when we should decline a nonpaying opportunity. Pamela Christian's excellent article on the topic of speaker's fees at the end of this chapter should help you as you develop or continue your speaking ministry.

Featured Author

    Pamela Christian   www.PamelaChristian.com

Featured Resources

Christian Speakers	www.christianspeakers.com
CLASS	www.classervices.com
Dedicated Author	www.groups.yahoo.com/group/ ededicatedauthor
Manna Conference Tapery, Inc.	www.mannatapes.com
National Speakers Bureau	www.nsb.com
Speak Up Speaker Services	www.speakupspeakerservices.com
Toastmasters	www.toastmasters.org
Women's Ministry.net	www.womensministry.net

Speaking to Promote Your Book

by Marita Littauer

Publishers today would rather publish an author who is marketable than publish a great literary work written by someone who is not marketable," was the opening I used in my introduction many years ago at the first writers' conference at which I taught. I shocked the audience, which was largely made up of introverted writers striving for literary excellence.

That first conference was held only days after the annual CBA Convention. While I was at the convention, I queried representatives of publishing houses of all sizes; and they confirmed the prognosis of my years of publicity work. Since then, the validity of my conclusion has only intensified, especially for those of us who write nonfiction.

If you attend a writers' conference today and have the opportunity to meet with editors about your book idea, one of the first questions they will ask is, "How often are you speaking?" Publishers know—speaking sells books.

Creating a Demand for your Book

Ask any speaker/author where the majority of their book sales come from, and they will tell you back-of-the-room sales, or what is known in the business as BOR. Think about the last time you went to hear a speaker/author at a conference. As you walked in the door, you probably passed tables displaying the speakers' books. You may have slowed as you passed and casually glanced at the titles available. Others followed suit as they arrived.

Marita Littauer is a professional speaker with over twenty-five years of experience. She is also the author of ten books, including *Personality Puzzle; Talking So People Will Listen; You've Got What It Takes;* and her newest, *Love Extravagantly.* She is the President of CLASSServices, Inc., an organization that provides resources, training, and promotion for Christian speakers, authors, and publishers. Through the CLASSeminar, Marita has trained thousands of Christian speakers and authors and launched many ministries. For more information on CLASS, visit www.classservices.com or call 800-433-6633.

But once the speakers are finished (assuming they did a good job and people liked them), the book table is swamped. It is difficult to get near to make your selections. Hours earlier, the books sat on display unwanted. But once people hear a speaker, they want the book on that topic. I recently heard that the books of one of the most popular women's speakers today don't sell if they are not about the topic on which she speaks. Most of her speaking opportunities showcase her humor. Her funny books sell. Her gift books, serious titles, and Bible studies do not. The lesson to all of us is: If you want to sell your books, you need to be speaking on those topics.

Additionally, bookstores report that an author's books continue to sell in the store for months after that person's appearance in the area. When I talked to a bookstore employee from a town I spoke in, she commented that everything I talked about sold well and my books continue to sell. When people hear your presentation and connect with your message, they buy your book. They then become fans of your work and go back to the bookstore looking for other titles you may have authored and spread word-of-mouth recommendations.

Letting People Know about You

Begin to establish your speaking ministry by creating your promotional materials. These do not need to be glossy brochures with embossed cutouts of you in a dramatic speaking pose. One computer-generated page will suffice.

Start by selecting a preprinted paper and font that represents your message and style. Include your biographical information, focusing on what God has done in your life that qualifies you to be an expert on your topic. List your available topics with clever titles and blurbs explaining the speeches. End with your contact information: name, address, phone number, e-mail address, and Web site.

Getting Those First Speaking Engagements

Once you have your promotional piece ready, you need to get it into the appropriate person's hands. Start by looking for local groups who bring in speakers. You can find many of these in your newspaper. Look for listings of churches that have upcoming programs that involve speakers, for example. They will need speakers for future events.

If your topic will work for general audiences, contact service clubs like the Rotary or Lions Clubs. Call the name and number listed in the paper. Ask for the name and number of the program chairman and contact him, telling him about your presentation. Usually, he will ask you to send your "stuff," which is why it's wise to create it first.

Two other avenues to garner speaking invitations are through your pastor and friends. Assuming you are active in your church and your pastor is supportive of your message, ask him to send a personal letter on church letterhead (which you will write for him, address, and pay for postage) to all his pastor friends. Most ministers have several sets of professional friends: those they went to seminary with, those in the state denominational board, and those in the local evangelistic association. The letter will give a glowing recommendation of your message and abilities, encouraging the recipient to invite you to speak at an appropriate church function. Be sure to include your promotional piece with the letter.

Next, send your promotional piece to all your friends with your Christmas card. Include an annual letter telling what different family members have been doing, including you. Let them know you have written a book and are now speaking on the topic. Suggest that if they need a speaker for their churches, you might be the right person. Ask them to pass your promotional materials on to the person in charge of events.

If you try these avenues for marketing yourself as a speaker—and if God wants you to speak—you will get invitations.

Selling Books on Site

At your speaking engagement, you have the privilege of getting your message into the hands of many people who will buy your book and pass it on to others who need it. Be sure the meeting planner knows ahead of time that you will be bringing books; that you will need some space to display them; and, if a friend is not joining you, you will need a volunteer helper who can assist you with the sales.

Before you pack up to go to the event, you'll need to know how many people will be attending to help you determine the number of books to bring. If you will be speaking on the topic of your book and you show it once or twice during the presentation or read a quote from it, so the audience makes the connection between the topic and the title, you can plan on selling to about 10 percent of the audience. If you are driving to the location, you may want to throw in some extra books since it won't cost you anything. However, if you are flying and have to ship books in advance, your zealousness can be costly. Whether the event is local or a flight away, it may be best to have your publisher drop ship your books to the venue. Call the customer service or author relations department, request the number of books you need, and tell where to ship them and by what date they must arrive. In general, plan to ship about two weeks before the speaking date.

Once you are on site, set up your book table with price signs or stickers that will allow customers to shop easily and help your volunteer know how much to collect. Be sure to have cash available for making change. (It is customary to give your helper and the meeting planner a copy of your book as a thank you.)

Assuming everything has gone as planned, you should now be out of books. However, if not, and you are flying home, hopefully—as is my goal—you have so few copies left that you can stash them all in your suitcase. Sometimes the final numbers were not as you'd been told to expect or you overestimated, leaving you with an extra case or two of books to get home. If the cases are the same size, you can tape two together (always carry packing tape), so the airline will count them as one to keep your checked baggage under the limit. If you are over the limit, ask your meeting planner to ship the excess books back to you; and cover the cost of the postage.

One last word of advice: While you may consider selling your books as a ministry, the IRS considers it a business. Check with a local accountant who specializes in small businesses regarding the rules and regulations of your city, county, and state; and file the appropriate forms and get the correct licenses to operate.

I am sure you can see that speaking and writing go together like a hand in a glove. But the greatest benefit is not the book sales. It is the message God has placed on your heart to share, so you can reach more and more people as your book gets passed from one person to another, touching and changing lives!

Speakers' Fees:
Considering the Costs

by Pamela Christian

What is your fee?" This question poses one of the greatest challenges for speakers, especially those who are launching a speaking career. Figuring out what to charge can be confusing, so I'd like to offer a few reasonable guidelines.

What Does the Bible Say?

Christian speakers' fees often are scrutinized differently from secular speakers' fees. The reasons for this discrepancy are varied and often unfounded when compared with Scripture. Some people, for example, emphasize Matthew 10:8: "Freely you have received, freely give." The context, however, includes the phrase, "for the worker is worth his keep" (v. 10).

Malachi 3:5 and Luke 10:7 provide additional support for reasonably compensating the Christian worker.

What Do the Workers Say?

Professional speakers have a lot to say; but on the topic of fees, many are closemouthed. Linda Evans Shepherd, founder of Advanced Writers and Speakers Association, explained, "I don't think speakers want others to know what they receive because there's concern that it will be viewed as an indicator of their professional level."

Another valid reason not to discuss fees is price fixing. The National Speakers Association, which boasts 4,000 members,

---

Pamela Christian's speaking and teaching ministry is powerful and has resulted in invitations to speak coast to coast since 1997. She is a staff member with CLASServices, Inc., and a member of Advanced Writers and Speakers Association. She and her husband, David, daughter, Rachel, and son, Gregory, reside in Yorba Linda, Calif. Learn more about Pamela at www.pamelachristian-ministries.com. Adapted from "Money and Ministry," a three-part series exploring professional Christian speakers' fees for conference planning.

instructs speakers not to discuss fees in a meeting with colleagues because doing so could be considered price fixing.

However, we need some guidelines. Marita Littauer, president of CLASServices, Inc. (Christian Leaders, Authors & Speakers Services), sheds some light on this topic. Although the following suggested ranges are specific to CLASServices, they are fairly typical of Christian speakers and meeting budgets. She explains that there are three basic categories of speakers and, therefore, three basic fee ranges.

Beginning speakers are those who are starting out and have no name recognition but who have already done many free presentations to hone their skills. Typically their work is local, and they cover their own travel expenses. The fee range for anything from a single message to a full weekend retreat is from $25 to $800, perhaps even $1,000.

For intermediate speakers, who have some name recognition but not enough to draw large audiences and whose work takes them across state lines, the range is about $800-$3,000, with travel, meals, and accommodations provided.

For well-known names, such as Florence Littauer, Lee Ezell, Kay Arthur, and Liz Curtis Higgs, whose speaking is international, the range is $2,500 and heavenward, with travel, meals, and accommodations provided in addition to the fee.

In contrast, general-market speakers are paid considerably more. Minimum fees for single messages or single-day events are often quoted between $2,500 and $5,000. Many of these speakers consider $10,000 for a weekend on the low end. Day-long corporate workshop planners pay around $15,000 to a speaker/trainer who is a draw or a "headline" name, such as Oliver North, whereas former President Bill Clinton requires $100,000. Whether general market or Christian, name recognition plays a large part in the speaker fee.

Speakers who are also authors often accept lower fees because a good portion of their income will be derived from on-site book sales. Even so, speakers should negotiate fees with others in mind. Brenda Nixon, a speaker and author, said this: "Speaking for me *is* my livelihood. I do not have a salaried position or 'real job.'

Therefore, I cannot do my craft for free. It hurts the rest of us when other people who speak on the side do it for an honorarium. Confused program planners naturally ask, 'Well if "So-and-So" spoke for free, why can't you?'"

Adding to Brenda's point, I know many speakers, even well-known ones, who occasionally commit for an amount unusually low for them. Their reasons are many, but the common thread in making that decision is an urging from the Lord to do so.

How Do You Set Your Fees?

Most speakers agree that 20 hours of work is required to produce a one-hour message. Obviously the same material used repeatedly makes it more cost effective for the creator; but virtually all messages are reworked for a new audience, requiring ongoing labor. Other behind-the-scenes expenses that impact fees include:

- Promotional materials: one-page flyer, photographs, business cards, brochures, Web site, and more.
- Postage: Shipping books to meeting locations is expensive.
- Demo tape: production, corrections, duplication, tapes, and cases. Tapes are sent free, and few are ever returned for reuse.
- Resale products: books, tapes, memorabilia.
- Professional labor: legal fees, accountant, bureau services, administrative help, editors, and publicists.
- Office equipment: computer, software, copier, fax, phone, and furniture.
- Licenses/fees: business license, sales tax, and professional fees.
- Research: resource materials, continuing education, and training.
- Insurance: medical, liability, and occasionally directors' and officers' insurance.
- Travel: luggage, containers, travel-agent fees, ticket-change fees, parking, and tips.

Above all, the most important question in deciding fees is: What does the Lord want me to do? Certainly our Lord does not want any of His own to be motivated by money. But when determining your speaking fees, remember Jesus said, "The worker deserves his wages" (Luke 10:7).

Chapter

Finishing Touches
Online (Internet) Promotions

The road to success is always under construction.
—Jim Miller

Before Homer arrived at the small Arizona convent in *Lilies of the Field*, the German and Austrian nuns wanted to learn English. Living on the outskirts of town, they had no one to teach them, so their lessons consisted of an instructional record of phrases they repeated in unison. It was slow going and not very effective, but little by little they persevered.

The movie features several delightful scenes where Homer holds English lessons. Instead of using the record, the nuns began to form a relationship with this man who spoke English. There was laughter and song and enthusiasm that made English easier for them to learn.

Could they have learned English with a series of records and canned phrases? Of course, Berlitz has made millions of dollars from selling language training tapes and CDs. But learning a language is more effective and enjoyable when you have formed a relationship with a native speaker.

Like learning a foreign language, selling books is all about relationships. From editors to distributors to bookstores to consumers we need to create relationships every step of the way. Doing it inexpensively, twenty-four hours a day, is the beauty of the Internet.

Last July I sold sixty copies of *Portraits of Huntington's,* but only three of them were sold to customers directly through the Internet—one through my Web site and two through Amazon.com. That might sound as if the Internet is of little value to me when it comes to selling books. In reality, fifty-seven copies sold because of my Internet relationships.

A dozen of those books sold at a writers' conference after I spoke and sang. The conference director found my Web site and was so impressed with the book, the site, and my knowledge of the subject that she invited me to speak and sing. By the way, none of those who bought my book had any interest in Huntington's until they heard me speak; but they would not have heard me had I not had a Web presence.

The remaining forty-five books were sold at a Huntington's Disease speaking engagement at the Guthrie Center in the Berkshires. I met the event organizer online through an e-mail discussion group and, as a result, was invited to speak. I can honestly say that close to 100 percent of every book I've ever sold has come about because of either my Web site or a relationship began in a chat room, e-mail discussion list, or message board.

I teach at many writers' conferences each year and tell my students that they must be willing to invest time and money into becoming adept at Internet marketing. If they only want to rely on what the publisher does and a few book signings here and there, they won't sell many books. If they self-publish their books, they need the Internet even more.

One chapter is not enough on the subject of Internet marketing. My book *WriterSpeaker.com* contains reams of helpful information, especially for those who have not familiarized themselves with the Internet. The resource section at the end of this chapter is filled with Web sites that will help you become comfortable with Internet marketing. Visit the sites, ask questions, and eventually you'll find the Internet a must-have tool to use to reach your customers.

In chapter two I shared the depressing news that there were 135,000 new books published in 2001. Considering this staggering figure, and with more titles hitting the shelves every day, is there any question that Internet marketing is not only a viable option but an absolute must for those wanting to get their books to readers?

That said, please don't exclude other marketing strategies and invest everything in the Internet. More than any other type of marketing, I've found the Internet requires an enormous amount of time and energy to be effective. Depending on your learning curve and topic, you might have better success speaking or using direct mail.

Let's say you have a local title about the history of a ministry or business that is of primary interest to those within a hundred miles from home. You are already a member of several organizations and have begun to participate and speak at their functions. You are active in your church and volunteer with several high-profile charities. You also have a network of retail store owners who are willing to take your book on consignment. You have a full-time job and children, and your marketing hours are limited.

Unless you can somehow manage to lengthen your day by three or four hours, your time might be better spent speaking to local groups, sending out postcards, doing book signings, and working on some of the ideas you'll find in the last chapter of this book. A Web site might be fun to have, and at some point you might want to put one together; but it won't pull the sales without the effort.

That doesn't mean you'll never want to use the Internet to supplement what you are already doing; it just means you'll want to weigh your options. For you, e-mail might be a way to strengthen those relationships you already have. Eventually you might want to work with online bookstores, use bulletin boards and message centers, or even create a Web site.

If, on the other hand, your book has broad appeal to anyone around the world, you'll want to learn as much as you can and use the Internet in every way possible to reach people twenty-four hours a day. Even before you create that Web site you're planning, there are ways to use the Internet to promote your book.

E-mail

E-mail has been around long enough that most of you probably can't imagine getting along without it. There are expectations and courtesies to be remembered when it comes to using e-mail, however. These include the obvious, such as using your spell checker, making sure you include your name, having a professional e-mail address, and not forwarding attachments without permission. E-mail is a great way to form relationships, but not if you're constantly upsetting people. To learn more about e-mail blunders to avoid you can read "The Don'ts and Dos of E-mail" on my Web site at www.writerspeaker.com/youcan.html.

Besides sending an e-mail message now and then, there are a number of ways to use e-mail to promote your book. Below are a few of those ways. Not each idea is appropriate for each book, but you'll probably find several perfect for you.

E-mail Discussion Groups

Whether you start one of your own or join an already active group, this can be a superb way to sell books. Discussion groups are simply a way to bring together people with a common interest to discuss what is of importance to them. Name a topic, and a list probably exists. If it doesn't, you can start one yourself. In the resource section at the end of this chapter, you'll find links to several companies that can help.

I've been on several e-mail discussion groups since 1995. These lists have helped me forge relationships; position myself as an expert; interact with others who should be interested in my books; and, most importantly, be there to help those in need. Two years ago I recognized a need for a support group exclusively for caregivers of those with Huntington's Disease. Only a caregiver for someone with this disease really understands what I have been or will be going through, so I set up HDCaregivers through Yahoo Groups. It cost me nothing except my time, but each day I communicate with caregivers who might want my books or know someone who needs them. I am also a member of four groups for writers and speakers and have sold many copies of *WriterSpeaker.com* as a result of interacting with them.

The key to promoting your book through discussion groups is not to be pushy. This type of marketing resembles friendship evangelism. Rather than preaching and beating the Bible over someone's head, it's usually more effective to be a friend and live a life that leaves the nonbeliever realizing there's something missing in his or her life. By being active, answering questions, and referencing your book and Web site when appropriate, little by little—if you're part of a targeted group—you will sell books.

Opt-in (Subscription) Information Mailing Lists

These topical mailing lists are usually free and provide information people can use. It's the reader who chooses to subscribe, rather than receiving spam, or unsolicited electronic junk mail. Unlike discussion lists, this type of communication is there to read but not respond to. There will often be links and ads designed to drive traffic to a Web site or toll-free number, so the reader can buy a book.

E-mail Courses

E-mail classes can be fee-based or free; and, as the name implies, e-mail is used to disseminate information and for any homework given. You can offer a course from your Web site, using an autoresponder to deliver your material in small chunks; or you can offer it without a site.

Articles for Electronic Magazines (E-zines)

Many e-zine publishers and site developers are hungry for good content. Getting published in only one high-profile e-zine can give you exposure to thousands of people. You might not get paid for your work; but even if you don't, it could mean book sales. Make sure you retain all rights, can submit and sell it elsewhere, and that you receive a generous bio and Web site link.

John Vonhof, author of *Fixing Your Feet: Prevention and Treatment for Athletes,* shares his experience of allowing his work to be used by someone else. "An agent/publicist who helped RailRiders, an adventure clothing company, had always been a proponent of my book; and I had allowed an excerpt to be put up on their Web site. That article on how to duct tape your feet is still one of the most visited pages on their Web site. His belief in my book gave me publicity that I could not have afforded on my own."

Most e-zine owners are always looking for fresh content written by experts. If you've written a book, you are an expert, so take advantage of it. E-zines have a quick turnaround from the time you submit the article until it's published, and they allow you to reach thousands of interested prospects at once. When considering if you want your work to appear in an e-zine, subscribe for a few issues to see what it offers. Ask the editor if he will give you a free ad or banner in addition to publishing your article.

Start Your Own E-zine

E-zines are designed to attract highly targeted readers. They can take an enormous amount of work, but they can also be effective. If you are the author of a nonfiction book targeted to a specific group of readers, this might be the perfect tool for you. Even if you are a fiction author, you can still use e-zines to sell books.

Award-winning author Cec Murphey has come up with an interesting way that allows both nonfiction and fiction authors to use e-mail to promote their books. Cec, author of *The God Who Pursues: Encountering a Relentless God* (Bethany) believes in letting family, friends, and other authors know about his books and ministry. He sends out a monthly e-mail message with his news and that of several of his friends. The first two paragraphs of his communiqué say it all:

> Why this? Why you? A decade ago, writers wrote books, pub-lishers published them, and writers went on to their next books. In recent years, publishers want authors to help pro-mote their projects. In an endeavor to find new ways to get the news out about what's happening in my life, and in the lives of some of my friends, we've put together this e-newsletter to share with you the latest in our writing-ministry lives.
>
> Once a month we will send you this update about recently released and upcoming books. If you would like to partner with us in our ministry endeavor, here are a few ways you can help. (1) Buy one of our books. (2) If you like what you read, tell several friends to spread the news. (3) Buy copies for friends. (4) Write a review on Amazon.com or Christianbook.com. You'd be surprised at how important this is to authors. (5) If you have any connections, help us set up media interviews, especially radio, or book signings. (6) Most of us are also Christian speakers. Contact us individually for more information. Perhaps you have another idea as to how you can help. I'd love to receive any comments from you.

The subject line of the newsletter reads "What's New with Cec Murphey and Friends" and the message includes a short paragraph about what each of the authors has done that month. This is not about what might be in the future but what is now. As Cec says, "Let's deal with what *is,* such as speaking appearances, reviews of your book, a two-sentence quote from a reader."

He doesn't send attachments because the fear of getting a virus guarantees some readers will not open the e-mail. At the bottom of each message is the suggestion that if people choose not to receive the newsletter, all they have to do is send a reply to be removed.

For Cec the subject line never changes, but each author joining with Cec in this endeavor changes the line to include his or her name. When I become part of this group, my subject will be "What's New with Carmen Leal and Friends." My news will come first, followed by news from Cec, followed by the rest of the group.

Cec suggests that each e-mail be kept short and include a picture of you and your latest book. He also suggests adding the title, subtitle, publisher, and price.

For Cec this is as much about helping others as it is about himself. More and more, publishers want authors to play an active role in the marketing of their books. In order to make the newsletter as fresh as positive, Cec sets deadlines that his friends need to meet to have something new included in each issue. If they don't meet the deadline, the previous issue's news gets repeated. Any of his friends can drop out at any time but are asked to notify Cec if they find they are no longer able to participate. For more information about joining Cec Murphy and friends, or starting your own network, e-mail Cec at c.murphey@attbi.com.

You can use Netscape Mail, Outlook, Eudora, or a similar e-mail client to produce your e-zine. For simplicity you might want to consider a free automated service, such as Yahoo or Topica. Of course, as we well know, there is no such thing as that proverbial free lunch; and advertising will be displayed at the end of each message sent. I own two lists and have yet to find an ad that I found off-color or intrusive. Most authors would rather spend their promotional dollars on direct mail, advertising specialties, and trade shows, so they live with the advertising.

Another option if you have a Web site and a knowledgeable Webmaster, is to create a list from your Web site and send your e-zine from there. This way you eliminate the advertising.

This is only one type of e-zine that might work for promoting your book. John Vonhof has had success in selling books through his e-zine. His article, "Making an E-zine Work for Your Book," is featured at the end of this chapter. It's filled with information you'll want to read as you consider this marketing tool.

E-zine Advertising

You might want to partner with others who are more established through their e-zines or newsletters. Thousands of e-zines are looking for advertisers; and if you have the time to browse directories, you'll find many e-zines that target your readers. Before you pay their asking price, offer to write for them in trade for the cost of the ads. If you do need to pay, find out their subscription base and talk to other advertisers to see what their responses have been.

Even if you have to pay a fee, it is usually $10-50 per classified ad; so depending on the circulation, that could be a minuscule cost per reader.

Once you have written an ad that pulls in traffic, you can expand your advertising to dozens or even hundreds of other e-zines, depending on your book. This method works best if you have a Web site where readers can learn more.

E-zine classifieds are easy to insert and have a quick turnaround time. You can purchase them one at a time to test the waters rather than being tied to a long-term contract.

Signatures

One of the most effective tips I can suggest is the use of an e-mail signature. A signature is a block of text that appears at the end of each message you send. At a minimum, it usually contains contact information, such as your name and e-mail and Web site addresses. E-mail programs, such as Outlook, Netscape Mail, and Eudora, typically have an automatic signature feature. In Outlook, for example, you can set up your signature by using the signature feature under tools. In Netscape Mail and other programs, the signature is usually set in the preferences.

Using this feature in your e-mail program means you don't have to cut and paste it into each message every time. A signature file is stored on your computer; and each time you start an e-mail message, the signature is added automatically, though you don't necessarily see it on the screen. Keep your signature short. No matter how tasteful, funny, or creative the message, people generally don't appreciate lengthy ones.

A fellow writer who is a member of the Fellowship of Christian Writers (FCW) recently wrote to thank me for adding my signature to my e-mail: "I have been meaning to write you for some time. I find it amazing how God works, and the people He puts in our lives for different seasons and reasons. I had never heard of Huntington's until last summer when a dear friend's father passed away after battling the disease for years. As you might have guessed, my good friend is already showing symptoms. When I joined FCW, I read your signature line and went immediately to your site. When I told my friend about your book, she let me know that it was on her bedside table and she read it often."

She went on to share that she didn't really know why she was writing except to let me know that I am reaching people with my ministry. My Web site has information about this disease that could help Melanie better understand her friend, and I have a second book she could buy as a gift. My signature opened a new world for a friend who wants to help.

I have three different Web sites with three distinct target markets. Depending on which group I'm communicating with, I will use one or a combination of the following signatures:

Carmen Leal: Carmen@Writerspeaker.com
Web site design, books and conference topics for writers and speakers
www.writerspeaker.com

Carmen Leal: Carmen@CarmenLeal.com
Touching Hearts; Changing Lives
www.carmenleal.com
Author of *Faces of Huntington's* and *Portraits of Huntington's*

Carmen Leal: Carmen@allaboutquotes.com
Do you use quotations in your writing and speaking?
Subscribe to our free Daily E-mail Quote service.
www.allaboutquotes.com/Daily.asp

Here are a few other ways to use the Internet to promote your book.

Guide Sites

With the ever-increasing number of Web sites in cyberspace, many of them virtually worthless, it gets hard to sift through and select those that will be most helpful. In an effort to drive traffic to their advertising based sites, guide sites were born.

A guide site, such as About.com and Suite 101.com, is divided into topical sections with each section hosted by a guide. The host scours the Internet to find Web sites and other online resources and pulls them together in one easy-to-navigate place. Guides also write articles about the topics they are assigned to. While the pay for being a guide is nominal, the control is great. A guide can, of course, suggest his or her Web site and book as resources.

If you have a written a book, you might want to consider becoming a guide. Simply visit the main site and see if your category is listed. If it's not, and you think you might have time to explore this option, ask if you can become a guide. If your topic is listed, see if the guide will link your Web site and book as suggested resources.

Submitting to Online News Services

The same reasons and guidelines I gave about sending hardcopy press releases and news stories exist for online news services. More and more media outlets are accepting e-mail submissions, which is good news for you.

A number of media search sites are listed in the resource section of chapter four. When you visit them, take a look at the number of e-mail addresses included. You can also call services and ask for e-mail addresses to build your own e-mail media pipeline. The same rules of professionalism apply with e-mail as with traditional mail.

Chatting

Last year I was on a writers' conference panel. The topic was effective promotions, and I was one of the experts brought to the conference to share what works online. During the question-and-answer portion of the workshop, someone asked what we thought of chat rooms.

Another panelist quickly decried the use of chat rooms as an effective promotional tool. After she had her say, which primarily focused on the flakes and crazies that are drawn to the Internet, I made my comments.

Yes, there are unsavory and questionable people online and in real life too. You need to use common sense when it comes to chatting. You'll also want to consider limiting yourself to chat rooms where there is a host or someone who enforces general rules of good behavior. Typically, rooms that have been created for those with a specific interest are safe and are of tremendous value in sharing information about your book on the same topic.

Chatting can take up an inordinate amount of time; so, though I rarely chat, I set a limit for myself when I do. I've seen God work in chat rooms where people are able to unburden themselves because of the security of anonymity. Suicides have been prevented and people led to Christ online.

Be careful about sharing personal information, such as your home address or phone number. Plus you might consider using a different name, called a screen name.

You can schedule chat book signings and readings, teaching, speaking engagements, and being a guest in one of your fan club meetings. Technology continues to change, and there are many more chat options than previously available. Instant messenger is another way to build relationships online. The software you need is free, and I've provided addresses in the resources section that will get you started.

Online Bookstores

Amazon.com was the first online bookstore, and there doesn't seem to be an end in sight for the creation of them. An ever-increasing number of people love the ability to log on, go to a site, choose a book, use a credit card, and within a few days get the book delivered. About.com has an extensive list of online bookstores at http://publishing.about.com/cs/onlinebookstores. The resources section of chapter 3 has a few of the better known sites to get you started.

While the online exposure is great and it's easy to tell listeners during a radio interview to get your book at Amazon.com or Walmart.com, there is a hefty price attached to that convenience. Online bookstores charge anywhere from 40 to 55 percent of the retail price for each book they sell. There's no doubt that cover artwork, back-cover copy, author interviews, and excerpts all help to sell books; but the amount you get per book might surprise you. Your publisher will make all those arrangements and decisions without any discussion with you. If you have published your own book, you'll need to weigh all your options and decide what is best for you and your book.

Web Sites

If you do even a perfunctory Internet search, you'll find dozens of articles about how to sell a published book. The vast majority of those articles discuss selling books through a Web site. Having a Web site is probably the single best way to promote your books online if—and this can be a really big if—you are willing to work hard and keep your site fresh. You'll also need to be a creative site marketer to build consistent traffic.

You should no longer question the need for authors to have a Web site. In my book *WriterSpeaker.com,* there's an excellent chapter on creating a Web site and another about online marketing. If you are new to the Internet or to creating Web sites, you might want to buy this book, so you are familiar with some of the concepts and terminology. Also a variety of Web sites are available to help you design your site.

An author's site is one of the most affordable ways to attract new readers, communicate with those already familiar with your work, sell your products, and announce your speaking engagements and book signings. Web sites can be of the static bulletin board variety; or they can have bells and whistles, such as audio and video clips. You will be limited only by your creativity, energy, ability, and budget.

A site that exists solely for the purpose of selling books is not nearly as well visited or effective as a site designed for education and communication. Your personality, your mission and the books you have written will most likely be your starting point for the design. Whether your purpose is to educate, persuade, entertain, or sell should be obvious from the front page and throughout the site. Actually, an effective site should do all of the above and more.

Stephen Bly, whose book *The Long Trail Home* (Broadman & Holman) won a 2002 Christy Award, knows the value of online marketing. He and his author wife, Janet, are always looking for ways to make their Web site reader friendly and interactive. What they are doing is working because they say this year they have had an increase in books sold from their site.

"We offer contests with free Bly books for prizes. We include photos that fans send us of themselves reading Bly books. We have an active Bly Book Discussion Group link. Through our discussion group, we offer private pages on our site that include early previews of new book covers, feedback on stories we're working on, and suggestions for names for characters. We pull from this pool candidates for book dedications."

Another writing couple also believes that Web site marketing drives book sales for both fiction and nonfiction titles. Ron and Janet Benrey, authors of *Little White Lies* (Broadman & Holman), have an inviting site where visitors can read sample chapters and reviews, sign their guest book, get a free bookmark, and more. They've done a great job of incorporating their Pippa Hunnechurch series into the site. Visitors can learn how to host an English tea, find recipes for English trifle and Christmas pudding, and learn about Chesapeake Bay and Chichester, England, both areas featured in the series.

According to Janet, their site has sold books. But it also acts as a calling card. "Not too many people know who we are; but we can send them a link to the site and they can see us and learn who we are. This has been especially useful when contacting writers' conference organizers. In fact, people have even found us by chance. A recent find was St. Martin's Ministries. They invited us to their author and silent auction back in March. It was successful for selling books because, as the bookseller put it, 'you have a captive audience.'"

Randall Ingermanson, author of the Christy award-winning novel *Oxygen* (Bethany) also believes in Web site marketing. Of course, it's not as easy as it looks to those who have not gone through the process of getting visitors to their site. As Randy says, "The nice thing about Web sites is that they're available from anywhere in the world, 365/24/7, representing you to anyone who's interested in your book. The bad thing about Web sites is that not very many people are interested in your book unless they already know about you. And if they know about you, why do you need a Web site to tell them who you are? Catch-22! The solution to this problem, I believe, is to load your site up with stuff people are interested in and which they can find using search engines."

Randy shares his strategy and how many different things he did to gain visitors and a following: "When I wrote my first book (nonfiction) on the alleged Bible codes, I put together a Web site with all the information I could find. I wrote book reviews of all the major Bible code books. I put links to other sites and asked them for links back. I wrote articles summarizing my thoughts on the codes. I started a free e-mail newsletter and put a sign-up form on my Web site."

Randy also added a page of information about some of his writer friends and other writers he admired but didn't know personally. He wrote blurbs about their books and added links to Amazon.com. But he didn't stop there. "I registered with Yahoo and some other search engines. When my novels got published, I put free chapters of them on my site. My site has over fifty pages of stuff, and most of it is not a direct pitch for my books. Pretty soon the search engines started sending me a lot of hits."

Randy says he gets about two hundred hits per day, and most of these are from people who type Bible code into Google.com. Only a few of them result from searches for his name. "Now here's the astounding thing," he explains. "A lot of my hits come from searches for other authors. For example, if you type Dee Henderson into Google, one of the top results is the page on my site titled "Dee Henderson." Likewise for Rene Gutteridge and Brandilyn Collins. I had no idea this would happen—I just wanted to put in useful information for people who wandered across my Web site. It turns out that that useful information, indexed by Google, brings people to my site."

Randy is putting sound Christian principles into practice, and it's working. "My theory is that the more you give away, the more people will come to your site. So I try to give away a lot, including three free chapters of every book I've written and free Bible code software I wrote for my first book.

Like Ron and Janet Benry, Randy has found that his site has been valuable for more than sales. "One direct benefit to me is that I include a link on my Web site so readers can e-mail me directly. One of my fans for my first two books turned out to be an enormous source of information for my third and fourth books about Mars. She lives in Houston, used to work for NASA, and just happened to know an astronaut I could interview. That was worth all the effort I put into my site."

Each of these authors believes in giving information away, making sites interactive, and working to keep the content lively and fresh. So what does an author Web site look like?

I read somewhere that a good site should enrich the user's experience and expand the imagination. There are many good sites on the Web; but I think we should stop at nothing short of excellent, and that means having a site with personality and purpose.

As a minimum, an author site geared toward selling books should include an attractive front page; a table of contents, usually featured as buttons or navigational links; easily accessible contact information, including e-mail and mailing address if appropriate; a bio or résumé; an author photo, preferably in color; book cover images; and ordering information.

Once those elements are in place, it's your call as to what else to include. Depending on your site's purpose, consider adding the following:

- writing samples (make sure you actually own the copyright before posting)
- links to related sites in your field
- frequently asked questions (FAQs)
- online bookstore
- book covers and descriptions
- book excerpts
- ordering information
- writing tips
- speaking or book-signing schedule
- speaking topics
- speaking tips
- audio or video file of a sample presentation
- autoresponders (send automatic messages on requested topics)
- topical newsletters
- contests

- chat rooms
- message boards
- search engine

Web-Site Marketing

I've already mentioned a number of excellent Web-site marketing tips, but here are a few more. Also check the resources section and "Web Design for Authors" at the end of this chapter for help with designing and creating your site. Whether you do all the work yourself or hire a professional, this article is a must-read.

Reasons to Come

Your Web site is not a brochure or bulletin board. It also should not be simply an announcement to sell books. An effective site is one where new, original, and useful content is uploaded often. Remember the features and benefits you encapsulated on your back cover? Think about them each time you add something new to your site. Position yourself as an expert, whether in your nonfiction subject matter or as an expert writer or speaker.

Adding content daily or weekly gives visitors a reason to return. Hopefully they will bring others with them; and, as a result of all those visitors, your search engine rankings will rise. I feature a daily e-mail quote service to subscribers but I also post that quote each day. People have told me they visit my site every day just to read my quotes. You might want to add daily or weekly quotes, tips, riddles, articles, how-to lists, and more to your site. Others can also write articles for you as you do for them to have vibrant content without working yourself to death. Keep the articles short to keep visitors coming back.

E-zines

I've discussed using e-mail for your e-zine, but you can also publish one on your site. You can send out an e-mail teaser directing readers to your site for the rest of the article. Hopefully when they come to read the rest of the article, they'll stick around and buy a book.

Chats, Forums, and Message Boards

Simple programming or preexisting chat rooms can make it possible for you to drive traffic to your site instead of using Yahoo or iUniverse as a chat room. Once people are there, they might stick around and see what else you have to offer.

Teaching from your site is another option. Offering online classes can help create credibility and get people visiting routinely.

You can also host reading groups, yours or an another authors, or talk about yourself and your books to your fans.

Forums are information outlets where people post questions and information for others to read and respond to. You can make your site a place people learn to depend on for information by adding a forum or discussion board. Bravenet.com has an excellent array of free Webmaster tools to help you set up one.

Web-Only Specials

People love a bargain, so consider a Web-only special. It might include free shipping or a discount and it could be a reason someone comes to your site. For instance, I travel on Delta Airlines frequently and try to always book directly on its site because it offers 1,000 bonus miles for doing so. From Delta's perspective, this process eliminates its need to pay a commission to a travel agent or a company like Priceline.com. It also keeps me on its site to learn more about cruises and vacations I might like to try. Authors, especially self-published ones, know you make more money from direct book sales than through a bookstore. Web-only specials may increase direct sales, which, as Martha Stewart says, is a good thing.

Links

You can add links of related, yet noncompeting authors, ministries, or services. You can also ask those people and companies to link to your site. This win-win promotional tool is free and easy to implement and typically drives traffic to your site. It also helps to raise you in the search engine listings.

Being linked on other sites is of tremendous value in playing the ranking game. If you offer strong content, you can usually persuade other site owners or Webmasters to link to your site. Look for other sites that have your customers and see how you can work together. I am linked to hundreds of sites through both my Huntington's Disease content and writing and speaking material.

I mentioned earlier that selling books is all about developing relationships. That is also true when it comes to developing a link network. I have many friends who have linked my site as a way to help me. You might consider adding a page of links to your site and then asking those you have linked to to reciprocate. To see my page of writer and speaker links, go to www.writerspeaker.com/WSlinks.html. If you'd like your link added, please e-mail me at Carmen@writerspeaker.com.

Giveaways

Chapters from your book, handouts used in your presentations, results of a survey from your site, and a specially created group of links only available by visiting are all items you can give away on your site.

Each time I speak I mention that my handouts are available on my site for those who either bought the tape or simply want to get another copy. I also share short stories, jokes, humorous lists, and poems I know people love. I post these and suggest people visit to download a free copy. I have sold books and CDs and booked speaking engagements because of people stopping by for a freebie. Once they get to my site and look around, they invariably stay longer than planned and often buy something, or at least bookmark the site for a return visit.

My husband and I have developed a piece of quotation management software for writers, speakers, pastors, and others who use quotations. Soon, we will offer a free download with two hundred quotes from all of our sites. It not only is a great giveaway to drive traffic to our sites, but it also is a great promotional tool for the software itself. We'll provide All About Quotes as a download from any site that wants to promote the software or have a free gift for site visitors. The trial version comes with a window that pops up the first time the software is opened. The message in the pop-up window says, "This software is offered free and with no strings attached, just like God's love and eternal salvation. To learn more, visit www.carmenleal.com/salvation.html." We suggest churches offer the software as a free download to encourage traffic. If you or your church is interested in offering All About Quotes on your site, visit www.allaboutquotes.com.

We'll also feature an online greeting card site for those who want to send free All About Quotes cards. The card site is sponsored by All About Quotes software and WriterSpeaker.com. Hopefully when people use the free service, they'll visit the sponsoring sites and purchase books, CDs, and software.

Site Bookstore

Many people buy books through personal Web sites; but even more buy them through major bookstores, such as Amazon.com,

BarnesandNoble.com and Christianbooks.com. Selling your book through a commercial site means it deals with accepting credit cards and filling orders. If your volume is small, that's probably the best way to go.

However, you can also sell books from your Web site by allowing visitors to send checks or by taking credit cards. There are costs involved if you go the credit card route, and you might find sales aren't worth them.

Over the last few years, companies have sprung up that make it more affordable to accept money over the Internet. One of the most well known is PayPal. Recently purchased by eBay, PayPal offers a quick, secure, affordable way to purchase items online.

I like to give customers as many options as possible for ordering books from my site. I take checks by mail for those who want an auto-graphed copy, have a toll-free number through my fulfillment house, and direct readers to my Amazon.com bookstore.

Amazon is not the only bookstore that encourages affiliations; but I have signed up for its associates program, and you can too. Once you sign up for your free account, you get a special customer code that you can add to your Web site. When visitors click on the link, it takes them directly to the Amazon page where your book is listed. Each time your book, or any book or item linked back to your site, is purchased, you get 5-15 percent commission.

You won't get rich off these checks, but they do add up. Amazon, in particular, is wonderful about reports. I can tell at a glance how many people visited Amazon from my site and what items they viewed and purchased. My bookstore has writing and speaking books, as well as books about Huntington's Disease.

Search Engine Rankings

You certainly want to have your site appear when people do a search on your book's topic, but it's a time consuming and complicated process. There are numerous books about search engine submissions and rankings, but just know that to achieve the high rankings will take some serious work.

As a minimum, you'll want to make sure your meta tags are in place and your key words well chosen. My article on Web design and creation following this chapter will help in this area. Of course, you will need to submit your site to search engines. You can do that on an individual basis, but you'll soon find out how much time it takes. Free site submission tools are available on the Web, or you can go to a fee-based service. It will typically offer to submit your site to hundreds or even thousands of search engines. This sounds good; but in reality there are fewer than a dozen to be concerned about, so you'll probably overpay. Several sites in this chapter's resource section will lead you in the direction for increasing your rankings.

Banner Ads

I know few authors who have successfully used banner ads as a way to promote their books. It's mainly the major search engines or sites that offer banner ads. It is possible to drive traffic to your site through banner ads, but you need to understand the way the game is played.

I personally find banner ads annoying and never click on them to learn more. Before spending any of your limited promotional dollars on banner ads, take time to learn more.

Classified Advertising

Most authors don't use online classified ads to sell their books; but, depending on the topic, you might want to consider advertising with AOL or Yahoo. AOL is still the number-one Internet service provider in the world. Its members are often fiercely loyal and stay on AOL rather than venture onto the Internet. AOL classifieds could be the way to reach those members. The key to success is to create a headline that makes your ad stand out above the hundreds of others in each category. For about the retail cost of one book, you can have your ad where millions of people will see it.

Yahoo also offers classified advertising. Since it has more traffic than any other site on the Internet, start there if you're going to try ads. On Yahoo, you are allowed to place ten free ads at a time. All it takes is time to create and submit the ad. If you delete your ads every few days and then replace those you have deleted, you can keep your ads at the top of the list where visitors are more likely to see them.

Offline Promotion

Promote your Web site offline, as well as on. List your Web site and e-mail address on your business card, letterhead, postcards, and other promotional material. When you are asked to provide a bio, cite your Web address and e-mail as a way of learning more about you, your book, or your ministry. When giving a talk or any sort of public promotion, such as a television or radio interview, encourage people to visit your Web site.

This is in no way an exhaustive list of online promotional ideas. Visit author sites, both Christian and secular, to see what others are doing to promote their books. Remember, online marketing can be effective; but it does take lots of time and should not be the only marketing tool you use.

Featured Authors

Janet and Ron Benry	www.benrey.com
Stephen and Janet Bly	www.blybooks.com
Randall Ingermanson	www.rsingermanson.com
Cecil Murphey	www.cecilmurphey.com
John Vonhof	www.footworkpub.com

Featured Resources

Book Price Comparison

ISBN.nu	www.isbn.nu

Chat Software and Sites

AOL Instant Messenger	www.aim.com/index.adp
ICQ	www.icq.com
Ircle (Mac)	www.ircle.com
iUniverse Chat	www.communities.iuniverse.com
mIRC (PC)	www.mirc.com
Yahoo	http://chat.yahoo.com
Yahoo Messenger	http://messenger.yahoo.com/ messenger

Christian Search Engines and Portals

Active Spidering Search Engines	www.active-ss.com
Acts Christian Web Search	www.actschristian.com/a
ChristianWebSite	www.botcw.com/index.html
Christian Add URL	www.christianaddurl.com
Christian Broadcasting Network	www.CBN.org

Christianlinks	www.christianlinks.com
Christianity Today Search	www.christianitytoday.com/search/index.taf
Christ Sites	www.christiansites.com
Christian Directory	http://search.711.net
Christians Unite	www.christiansunite.com
Cross Canada Search	www.crosscanadasearch.com
CrossDaily.com	www.crossdaily.com
Cross Search	www.crosssearch.com
CrossWalk	www.crosswalk.com
Everything Christian	www.everythingchristian.org
His Net Christian Directory	www.his-net.com
iChristian Web	www.ichristianweb.com
iBelieve.com	www.ibelieve.com
InJesus	www.injesus.com
Light Links	www.lightlinks2000.com
Pastors.com	www.pastors.com
Praize	www.praize.com
Religious Resources	www.religiousresources.org
Rob's Christian Links and Search Engine	www.robslinks.com
Ultimate Christian Resource	www.chritech.com
Worthy Links	www.worthylinks.com

Electronic Magazines and Newsletters

Directory of Ezines (fee)	www.lifestylespub.com
Ezine Ad Auction	www.e-zineadauction.com
EzineLocater.com	www.e-zinelocator.com
Ezine Universe	www.ezine-universe.com

Guide Sites

About.com	www.about.com
Suite 101.com	www.suite101.com

Mailing Lists

CataList	www.listserv.net/lists/listref.html
Christian eMail Service	www.christiane-mailservice.com
Internet for Christians	www.gospelcom.net/ifc/mail/view/?ifc

Tile.net	http://tile.net/lists
Topica.com	www.topica.com
Yahoo Groups	www.yahoogroups.com

Media Searches
See pages 77, 110-111

Online Bookstores
See page 56

Online Classifieds

AOL	www.aol.com
Yahoo	www.yahoo.com

Online Payments

PayPal	www.paypal.com

Web Tools

Bravenet.com	www.bravenet.com
Jim Tools	www.jimtools.com
iWeb Webmasters Toolkit	www.jimtools.com
Search Engine Guide	www.searchengineguide.com
Search Engine Watch	www.searchenginewatch.com

Making an E-zine Work for Your Nonfiction Book

by John Vonhof

The Internet allows anyone with a nonfiction book to create an e-zine, an electronic, web-based or web-distributed newsletter, to promote his or her title. In eight months my e-zine, with the same title as my book, *Fixing Your Feet,* has gone to almost 500 subscribers. After subscribing to about 30 e-zines of different topics, I had a good feel for their benefits.

I studied the Internet for e-zines whose format I liked and made a template. Deciding to write one editorial each month required I find someone to contribute another article, and I would fill the rest of the e-zine with tips and hints, new product reviews, and quotes—all about foot care. Within the e-zine is one ad for my book, directing readers to my Web site; a second short piece asking readers to post a review on Amazon.com if they have found the book helpful; and a note asking for feedback and that they pass the e-zine along to others. I create the content in TextPad® (shareware at www.textpad.com) to control the line length and make it uniform to fit with all major browsers.

I chose Yahoo Groups (www.groups.yahoo.com) to host my e-zine because they are free and require virtually no owner maintenance. All subscribers have to opt in, meaning they subscribe and then have to respond to a verification e-mail. This assures the e-zine owner of readers who want to read it and avoids spam complaints. As I find items of interest to my readers or contact a potential contributor, I drop a note into a file folder. Once a month I open the folder and pull out all the material. I write the e-zine, copy and paste it into the window in my Yahoo Groups home page, and hit "Send" to distribute it to all my subscribers at

John Vonhof is the author of *Fixing Your Feet: Prevention and Treatment for Athletes.* To subscribe to his e-zine or learn more about his book, visit www.footworkpub.com.

one time. Then I record the titles of the articles and a list of the tips and products mentioned, so I don't repeat them too soon.

My e-zine has given my book worldwide exposure; given me added credibility as an expert; and puts my name, my Web site, and the book's title in front of all e-zine readers *every* month—all for free. Every e-mail message I send carries my signature with links to subscribe to my e-zine and the home page for Footwork Publications (my company). The title page in my book also carries my Footwork Publications URL and a link to subscribe to my e-zine.

Does it pay? In the past few years, e-zines have sprung up on every conceivable topic, including many nonfiction books. E-zines are big business. While I cannot point to any concrete numbers, I know my book is receiving greater exposure; and I am constantly offering my readers something new. Without an e-zine, your readers have to hold your book in their hands or see it on their shelves to be reminded of you. With an e-zine, my readers are reminded of seven things: the name of the book; the value of the book; my name; my name reinforced in their minds as an expert; new articles, ideas, or products related to a topic they have interest in; when the next edition is coming out; and a direct line to talk to me. I'll take that added value when it only costs me a few hours each month. Will you?

Web Design for Authors

by Carmen Leal

If a site would be a useful addition to your marketing plan, you need to determine how best to make it happen. Creating a Web site is not rocket science, but there is a learning curve. There are do-it-yourself books and sites, that can either help or confuse, and any number of site designers who would love to help you.

In between those two options is doing it yourself. Like many of you aren't speakers, a good number of you are not technologically inclined; and taking on the challenge of creating your own site might be more than you care to handle.

If you do decide to do it yourself, there are many tools that can help. In the resource section at the end of this article as well as this chapter, I've listed Web sites that can help you as you begin the process.

WYSIWYG (pronounced WIZ-ee-wig), is an acronym for the phrase *what you see is what you get*. A WYSIWYG editor (program) allows you to create a Web page that lets you see what the end result will look like while the interface or document is being created. A WYSIWYG editor is a quick way to create a site without learning HTML. HTML stands for hypertext markup language. It really is a simple programming language compared to other more robust ones, but it still takes time to learn.

Newer versions of Netscape and Microsoft® Word come equipped with a WYSIWYG if you don't want to spend additional money on software. After reading the product reviews, you can decide if investing in a stand-alone editor makes sense for you.

Beatrice Gormley decided she needed a Web site and, after trying to work with a volunteer Webmaster, went another route. She's not alone in what she's dealt with as I've heard variations of her story from many authors. "My first Web site was set up for me a few years ago as a favor by my husband's nephew's wife. I liked my site, and I got a lot of compliments on it; but I became increasingly frustrated at not being able to update the site myself. For every little thing, I'd have to send the changes—text and any new pictures—to my Webmaster and wait for her to get around to making them. It could take months to get a page about a new book on my site."

Beatrice goes on to share how unacceptable that was since no one can afford to wait months, or even days, to promote a book. She wanted a tutorial from the Webmaster; but with one in Massachusetts and the other in Colorado, that never happened. As with many Webmasters, this wasn't her day job, so Beatrice's site got pushed further and further down her list of priorities. Hoping that offering to pay for the job would help, she did so.

"I felt uneasy about this and offered to pay her, asking her to tell me what her fees were. She just said she was glad to manage the site for me—and if I'd like to send her a check from time to time to contribute to the cost of her software, that would be great. So I did send her a check from time to time, but I never knew whether it was enough, too much, or stingy."

Things went from bad to worse when her Webmaster became her husband's nephew's ex-wife. Eventually Beatrice decided something had to give if she wanted an up-to-date Web site.

"When the Authors Guild, to which I've belonged for years, began offering Web site hosting, complete with a user-friendly site builder (no need for me to learn HTML code), it sounded exactly like what I wanted. By this time I had my own fax/scanner, so I could scan book covers and photos that I wanted to put on my site."

The Author's Guild is one of many places where a writer can get an affordable, or even free, hassle-free site. Of course, there are only a few templates offered; so your site might end up looking like other author sites. You'll have to decide how much creative influence you want in your site design, but this is one way to have an author site.

Many authors have chosen to work with someone already well versed in creating Web sites, rather than investing a lot of time in learning a new skill. When I teach at writers' conferences, I am often asked how much an average site should cost. There are too many variables to give you an average cost; but like any service, it pays to do your homework before spending your money.

I recommend making a list of sites you like, both author sites and others, and sending an e-mail to the site owners. A few questions might be all it takes to find the right designer for you. Ask them who designed their site and if they were happy with the service; who came up with the design; who provided the graphics; how long it took; and, if they are willing to tell you, how much it cost. If they are willing to share the cost, find out if it costs extra maintenance.

Once you have several designers to choose from, send them an e-mail message, inquiring about their services and rates. Visit their Web sites and learn as much as possible about the way they do business. Ask them for a minimum of three clients you can e-mail and ask the above questions. Regardless of who you hire, always ask for a contract.

My husband, a Web designer and programmer with over twenty-five years experience, specializes in creating sites for writers and speakers. We have an all-inclusive package that works well for most writers and speakers. You're welcome to visit our design site at www.writerspeaker.com/design.html and read our contract and use it as a guideline for whatever designer you hire.

A Web site is more than pretty pictures and text pulled together for visitors to see. Once you have determined your site's focus and your goals, you have a starting place. Site design includes not only the look and feel, but also the functionality. When my husband, Gary, designs or evaluates a site for clients, they work together to create a unique look that incorporates the author's personality, books, and mission.

Besides the basic attractiveness of a site, Gary makes sure the site is functional and easy for visitors to find. A few months ago I heard about a new novel with Huntington's Disease in the plot line. I wanted to communicate with the author and offer to do a book review for him, so I did a search to find his Web site. I searched for close to an hour. Although I found his book listed on many Web sites and bookstores, I couldn't find his personal site.

I finally wrote to his publisher, asking for an e-mail or Web site address for him and received his site address. After a quick look at the site, I knew exactly why I couldn't find it in a search. It was obvious the author had paid a professional to create the site, and it was attractive. The navigation was fine, and there was lots of information. There was also a big problem. The designer had made the site as an image map. Instead of being a combination of text and pictures written in code that was easily indexed by search engines, the designer had simply taken all the components and made one large image. The author had a Web site; but unless you knew the address, you couldn't find it because search engines don't index image maps.

Web Site Basics

It's impossible to give you everything you need to know to design a site. Instead, what I've tried to do is give you guidelines to get you started. In addition to the suggestions listed below, there's a ten-point site evaluation worksheet on my Web site that will help you or someone you hire put together an effective site.

As you get started, follow these guidelines:

- Your site should have a clear, easily recognizable focus.
- The information should be easy to find and easy to use.
- The design should be appealing to its intended audience. A children's book site might be whimsical and fun, while a business book site might be more serious.
- Backgrounds should not overwhelm the text. Pictures and graphics should be of the highest quality possible, and any animated graphics should have a specific purpose and not be distracting.
- The site navigation system should be obvious, and visitors should be able to easily find their way around the site.
- The content should be well-organized and broken into categories versus being on one or two long pages. Every page should be user friendly, and all links should work. The content should be well written and give visitors a reason to make repeat visits.
- The design should reflect your personality, mission, and brand and be appropriate for the intended audience.
- To ensure that all pages load as quickly as possible, all graphics should be sized and optimized for speed.
- A link to the contact information should be found easily on each page.
- Your site should be constructed to be easily indexed by search engines. A variety of well-chosen description and

meta tags should be included on all pages. Unless you or a professional designer understands how to program for indexibility, avoid using frames and image maps.

It's important to remember that creating and maintaining a Web site is a process. Later you can add links to other sites of value to your readers, a search engine, a subscription newsletter or e-zine, new content, and other items to enhance your site.

Whoever designs your site should view each page on both a PC and Mac, using different versions of both Netscape and Internet Explorer. Not everyone uses your operating system or browser; and pages may look different, depending on the browser, operating system, and settings. Finding out how your pages look to others will help you create a more universal site.

Another thing to remember is that even if you choose fonts to create the look and feel that's right for you, not everyone has those fonts. By adding a common default font, you have more control over how your site looks to those who don't have your preferred font.

Regardless of your topic and specific design, the content must be easily understood and deemed valuable to your target audience. Obviously your writing needs to be grammatically correct, properly punctuated, and spelled correctly.

A Web site designed to sell a book should focus on the book without deviating from your topic. Include adequate information and links to make visitors feel the site is worth recommending to others. I've seen too many sites that mix content and end up trying to meet the needs of many people, but come across as disjointed.

I now have three unique sites, each with its own distinctive, yet related look and feel. A link to the other sites is featured on each page, but the content on each is original. The site to promote this book and *WriterSpeaker.com* has information about my books, of course; but it also has articles and links for writers and speakers. My company site has a focus on Huntington's Disease and my other nonwriting speaking topics, and I have a third site to promote our quotation management software.

Remember that 80/20 rule we discussed earlier? Amazingly the same rule is true for Web sites. Putting up the page is easy, making sure it's maintained with new content added on a regular basis is time consuming. It's also effective.

Naming Your Site

In most cases an author's name is the perfect choice for a domain name. If your name is already taken, you can always use your middle initial or go with .net or .org instead of .com. If for some reason you decide to use a name other than your own, remember that choosing the right domain name for your Web site is essential if you want an effective site.

The name should explain what your site contains and, equally if not more important, it should be a common word, so people can remember it easily. Choose a name that will also serve as a keyword for the site, so the search engines will show it when people search for sites like yours.

Graphics

Besides making your page slow to load and possibly irritating, there's another reason to avoid too many graphics. Search engines read only text and images, and a page with too many graphics and little text is almost negligible to a search engine. There are ways to design a graphics heavy page more efficiently, and a good designer will know the tricks. But the best way to make sure your graphics aren't a hindrance and to make a pleasing page is to use a balance between the two.

A Search-Engine Friendly Site

I've stressed the importance of content, but in reality the most important words on your site aren't seen by your visitors. A description tag is a concise sentence or two used to describe your site. This is what is seen in the search result when your site comes up after someone does a search on Yahoo, Google, or another search engine. If there is no description tag present, the first text on your first page will be what the reader sees as a site description.

Keywords are a type of shorthand used by search engines to index your page. They describe your page and what makes it unique and different from others on the Web. The words you select should also appear throughout the text on various pages.

Make sure they appear in main headings and section headers. Also plan your paragraphs, so keywords appear somewhere in the introduction, content, and conclusion sentences.

Keywords should be as specific as possible. If you must use popular keywords because that's what your page is about, combine them with other words to make phrases that people might search for. Your keywords can be single words or two- or three-word phrases separated by a comma. Also use a few synonyms of the keyword in your text. The idea is to use keywords that are common enough so the typical searcher might use them, but unique enough to avoid millions of pages being returned in a search result.

Search engines ignore the most common words. These are called "stop words" because the engines don't bother to stop to read them. They typically ignore adjectives and articles, so don't rely on them as critical keywords on your page.

If no one can find your site using search engines, then you limit not only possible sales, but the impact you can make in people's lives. The best way to get higher search-engine placement is by registering your own domain name. At the end of this section are several domain registration and hosting companies where you can find low prices and excellent service.

Once you decided to write for publication, everyone told you to polish your writing skills and be the best writer possible. It's the same with ensuring your site gets consistently high search-engine rankings. If you develop excellent content, then people will be more likely to return to your site and encourage others to visit. The more traffic your site has, the higher you rise in the pecking order.

I'll conclude with two final words of caution. Whether you design your site yourself or hire a professional, make sure you keep a written record of your hosting company, user name, and password. We have had the unfortunate experience of an author not being able to access his site to make changes because he didn't have his user name or password, and the person who set up the site has disappeared.

The other caution is to make sure your e-mail address is current with the registration company. Renewal notices are sent to the e-mail on record; and if you have changed your account, the notice will never reach you. Many domain names have been claimed by someone else because people didn't know it was time to renew. Make sure you know your domain's expiration date and that you renew it at least thirty days in advance, so there's no confusion and you keep your identity.

Before you start creating what has the potential to be one of your most powerful marketing tools, study other sites. Keep it simple, easy to navigate, and interactive. Your home page should be where you spend the majority of your time and effort and consider your site visitors every step of the way.

Last of all, a Web site is only one way to market books, so pace yourself. As you begin or continue the design process, don't neglect other opportunities.

Recommended Resources

Domain Registration

    GoDaddy   www.godaddy.com

Hosting Services

Author's Den (free)	www.authorsden.com
Authors Guild (fee)	www.authorsguild.com
Christian Web Host (fee)	www.christianwebhost.com
ChurchSites (fee)	www.churchsites.com
Cornerstone Hosting (fee)	www.cornerstonehosting.com
Flock Hosting	www.flockhosting.com
FutureQuest (fee)	www.futurequest.com
Half Price Hosting (fee)	www.halfprice.com
HomewithGod (free)	www.homewithgod.com
Our Church (free)	www.ourchurch.com
Truepath (free & fee)	www.truepath.com
Wolf Digital	www.wolfdigital.net/ hosting.htm

Association
The Christian Webmaster's
    Association   http://cweb.gospelcom.net

WYSIWYGS
About.com   http://webdesign.about.
                                   com/compute/webdesign/
                                   msubeditors.htm

Web Site Tools
Bravenet   www.bravenet.com
C/NET   www.cnet.com/software/
                                       0-8172.7-309066.html
Pico Search Engine   www.picosearch.com
Search Engine Registration   www.uxn.com/
                                       search_engines.html

The Chicken's Guide
    to Site Promotion   www.guide.bloonatic.com

Section Three

Finding the Right Subcontractors

Credentials and Credibility
Working with Professionals

I always wanted to be somebody. If I made it, it's

half because I was game enough to take a lot of

punishment along the way and half because there

were a lot of people who cared enough to help me.

—Althea Gibson

In *Lilies of the Field,* Homer has to make a choice. Either he will stay and build the chapel, or he will leave. If he stays, he knows he can't continue living on the minimal meals served by the nuns out of their meager budget. If a man does physical labor, he needs to eat; so Homer hires on as an earth mover two days a week with a local contractor. The other three days he builds the chapel.

Whether you have a day job or not, there are many other activities and commitments that get in the way of your writing and marketing. You might resent not being able to invest more time in selling your book, but you can't drop everything else. Life continues even after publishing a book.

Eventually Homer begins building the chapel. He takes pride in his efforts, not just pride, but unreasonable pride. Homer decides he can do everything himself and doesn't need any help from anyone. After all, God has chosen Homer to build Mother Superior's "shapel."

Village people, so happy they were finally getting a church, walk miles to the site and begin to help. Women mix adobe, and men start helping with the construction. Homer wants none of their help, however, and chases them all away. The people sit and watch and wonder why they aren't being asked to use their considerable skills to make their dream come true.

When Mother Superior confronts Homer, he says, "You prayed up a lot of bricks, Mama. But you only prayed for one man to build your chapel."

Eventually the people get tired of doing nothing and begin to do a little here and a little there. So Homer stomps off to sulk. "I wanted to build it myself. I don't want any help. I wanted to build it myself. See, all of my life I wanted to really build something, you know."

Because Mother Superior is a straight shooter, she says, "God is building up there the chapel. You sit here feeling sorry for yourself because you are not Him."

Without a leader and a focus, the villagers make many mistakes; and the project begins to fall apart. Finally Homer realizes his role is not to construct the church alone. As Juan says, "Every job needs a boss who knows what he is doing."

Self-sufficiency is the enemy of God's people. Ephesians 4:16 tells us, "From him the whole body, joined and held together by every supporting ligament, grows and builds itself up in love, as each part does its work." And 1 Peter 4:10 says, "Each one should use whatever gift he has received to serve others." Even though we have read God's infallible Word, we still like to depend on ourselves, rather than ask for—or even pay for—help.

In the first chapter, I talked about making God your Master Builder. As Juan said, every job needs a boss; and that person should always be God. However, every job also needs a foreman, or an overseer, and that's you. Successful marketing starts with understanding your gifts and how you can use them to get your book to readers. But it is of equal importance to understand where you don't have gifts and who you can hire to help you achieve your goals.

In any building project there is a contractor, foreman, and crew. In your case, the personnel include God, you, your publisher, and others who have made your book a reality. A contractor hires a lot of other people to do other work to complete the job. These individuals, or sometimes companies, are called subcontractors. Plumbers, electricians, flooring experts, painters, and other specialists are called in to do what they have trained for to complete a portion of the project.

It's important to know when you can handle a job or when it's better to use a subcontractor. Some of the key people you might want to consider using are distributors, fulfillment houses, graphic designers, printers, mailing-list vendors, libraries, media consultants, promotional services, speakers' bureaus, and Web designers. The resource section at the end of the chapter features Web sites you can explore to find key companies to help in your marketing efforts. Be sure to ask for referrals and do the research to make sure you've chosen the right suppliers.

Distributors

One of the first lessons an author needs to learn is that there is a book publishing food chain. People do buy books from bookstores—though as I've already indicated, not exclusively—or for some books, not at all. Bookstores do not typically buy books from authors. Yes, self-published authors can approach a bookstore directly, set up book signings, and sell books on consignment. They can even get their books into the system that way, but it's not the norm.

Bookstore managers don't usually buy books from publishers. Instead, they buy from distributors. This way they pay one invoice to the distributors instead of to each author or publisher represented on their shelves.

Distributors are only one of the middlemen inherent to the system. According to Dan Poynter in *The Self-Publishing Manual,* "Distributors act as the fulfillment department for their publishers. More publisher-driven, their mission is to create orders from stores" (Para Publishing, 9th ed., p. 260).

If your book has been self-published, you're in an awkward position. Major distributors, the ones the major bookstores use, won't take your book. Of course, those are the distributors with sales reps, catalogs, and influence designed to create a demand for your book.

There are a number of smaller, reputable distributors who will accept your book, however. The trick is to match your book with the right distributor. Just as there are niche books, there are niche distributors. A company specializing in computer books would most likely not be interested in—and not do a good job with—a relationship book by a

Christian author. The key is to find a distributor who has already built relationships with those who are more likely to order your book.

You'll want to make sure your book is manufactured no differently than any book published by a major publisher. This includes the cover design, printing, bindery, and, of course, the writing.

Distributors need to know if there are any advertising dollars being spent that will get the book noticed by bookstores and libraries. Most independent publishers can't afford to advertise their books, but you can always go the co-op advertising route with other authors. Just because you aren't going to advertise, it doesn't mean a distributor will say no to your book; but it does make it more challenging.

Ultimately distributors need to feel comfortable that your book has the potential to move off of bookshelves. If you have written a Christian book, you should consider going with a Christian distributor. If your book is turned down and you think a distributor is key to reaching your goal, then ask another and another until you find one that's a good fit.

Most distributors work on a consignment basis and pay for books sold ninety days later.

This is not the best news for writers. But it's the system; and you're not going to change it, so you'll have to live with it.

The distributor of this book is FaithWorks, which may consider your books. You can also review the list in the resource section for more distributors that might be perfect for your book.

For more information on distribution, independent publishers might want to read *The Self-Publishing Manual* by Dan Poynter or *Jump Start Your Book Sales* by Marilyn and Tom Ross.

Wholesalers

Wholesalers are basically warehouses for bookstores. With such a huge number of books in print, it's impossible for a bookstore to carry even a small percentage of them. Unless it's a best-seller or highly publicized book, a title they do carry will often be in a small quantity to avoid taking up valuable shelf space. A wholesaler allows the bookstore to order books electronically or by phone, often within twenty-four or forty-eight hours, eliminating the need for the store to maintain its own warehouse.

Fulfillment

Fulfillment includes maintaining an inventory; so when an order comes in, the books can be invoiced if payment is not included, packaged, and shipped. When an order is received, the customer's name is put into a database to grow a mailing list. Of course, if you're going to mail books yourself, you'll need mailing supplies, including boxes or padded envelopes, mailing labels, and postage.

You don't need to be a rocket scientist to get your book from your home office to someone's house, but it does take time. Most of the hard costs can be passed on to the customer in the form of shipping and handling fees, but your time is valuable. If you are like most authors who publish their own books, you should be able to do this step yourself. *The Self-Publishing Manual* has an informative section on order fulfillment that will help you determine if it is something you're comfortable doing and, if so, how to do it well.

If you don't take credit cards because your volume is not large enough to justify the cost, or if you simply can't be bothered to deal with this aspect of publishing, you might want to consider using a fulfillment house. Like wholesalers, fulfillment companies order your books on consignment and take a percentage of each book as compensation. It can be as high as 55 percent, but they do all the work and send you a monthly or quarterly check.

For that price, companies should offer a twenty-four hour toll-free number. They should also give you the contact information for every customer who has bought your book, so you can add it to your database.

Fulfillment houses do not drive sales to individual consumers or bookstores. They process the orders after you have created enough interest in your book. I do not have a distributor for my Huntington's Disease titles. I sell the overwhelming majority of books directly to the consumer via my Web site and speaking engagements. I like having a toll-free number for when I do radio or television interviews; and I also like being able to offer credit cards via Amazon.com and my fulfillment house, Book Clearing House.

Library Sales

The library market can be as difficult to break into as bookstores. Libraries include public, private, schools and universities, and government. Like bookstores, libraries use distributors that are familiar with their needs. The best way to get into a library is to get a distributor who knows the library market. I use Quality Books for my Huntington's books, but there are others that might take your book too.

Author and librarian Judy Gann shares her knowledge in "Marketing to Public Libraries" at the end of this chapter. That, along with a list of library distributors, should give you all you need to get started pursuing this market.

Catalogs

Getting your book listed in a catalog can expand your exposure and sales. Topical nonfiction books are excellent for catalog sales, which market directly to those interested in your book's topic.

You may think only large publishers can get their books into a catalog, but John Vonhof has firsthand experience of being in a catalog called RailRiders. "RailRiders makes clothes for athletes, and their catalogs carry articles about athletes who are 'movers and shakers' in the sporting world. In the spring of 2002, I was featured in the RailRiders clothing catalog as "The Mr. Fix-It of Footcare," with a personal interview, a photo of me patching a runner's feet, a cover shot of my book, an offer to readers to order the book through the catalog, and an invite directing readers to my Web site to subscribe to my e-zine. I had initially been skeptical about the idea, unable to see myself in a catalog that featured athletes making a difference. But I did the interview anyway." According to John, the catalog goes to over 20,000 readers. Publicity like that is priceless and has increased his sales.

John's success didn't come overnight. He worked hard to create a unique book, and little by little people began to look to him as an authority on his topic. He created a Web site, began speaking, writing articles, getting library sales, and doing anything else he could to sell books.

You might already be aware of catalogs that are a good fit for your book, but you can always find more. Depending on your book, you'll want to search the *Catalog of Catalogs* (most libraries have a reference copy available), trade journals, and associations. The Internet has a treasure trove of catalog sites; several are listed at the end of this chapter to get you started.

Catalogs are seasonal, sometimes for a quarter, a year, or another duration of time. They are time sensitive, but they reach huge numbers of potential buyers. More importantly, catalog buyers are targeted buyers. You probably couldn't afford to send even a postcard to a small percentage of that number.

Of course, your book will not featured for free. You could pay up to 50 percent per book sold, but you typically sell your books by the case and as nonreturnable. These are often sales you wouldn't have gotten in any other way, so it might be worth the effort it takes to find catalogs that are a good fit. Contact them via their Web sites, phone numbers, or addresses to find out how to get your book included.

Bulk sales, special licensing deals, and premium sales are other ways to sell books. If you're interested in pursuing these outlets you'll want to pick up a copy of *1001 Ways to Market Your Book* by John Kremer (Open Horizons).

Mailing Lists

Whether you're sending postcards, brochures, or a letter, the best results are achieved when the list is highly targeted. Your Christmas card list, alumni directory, or Rolodex™ contain the names and addresses of individuals who know you and have a better chance of being interested in something you've written. Topical lists from associations or special interest groups, too, have a higher success level than simply sending something to a general list.

So where do you find these great lists? Hopefully you've already started compiling your own personal list, but you might not want to stop there. Depending on your topic, there are lists you can compile yourself or buy from a list broker.

Compiling lists means culling through yellow pages, newsletters, school and association directories, and other places where names and addresses are listed and finding those that might be interested in your book. It's time consuming but can be quite effective. If you've written a book of interest to Christian counselors, or a title about homeschooling, then you should be able to create a solid list of leads.

The beauty of direct mail is that regardless of what you send, you can test market small batches, wait for the response, change your piece if desired, and send out more if you think it will work. If you decide to send more than two hundred pieces of mail, you'll want to consider sending them bulk mail. The U.S. Postal Service Web site has information on requirements and pricing. You'll need a permit, and you might decide to hire a direct-mail firm to process the mailing. To find a firm in your area, check the yellow pages under direct or bulk mailing.

You can also buy lists that target by zip code, education, income, interests, and more. These are usually priced per 1,000 and can be expensive. In general, the more targeted the list, the more expensive it is. Lists are sold for one-time use, either as labels or a computer database. A bulk mailing house will affix labels or print names and addresses from the computer file directly on your mailing pieces, process them for the post office, and bill you for the entire job.

The resource section has some mailing lists options; local list brokers can give you even more choices. Your public library either has or can have sent to it the *Direct Mail List Rate & Data*. This directory lists just about every mailing list that is available.

You can also create your own list of media who might be interested in your book. Several Web sites listed at the end of the chapter allow you to search by city and state or other parameters. You can build a list that way, or buy an existing database. Either way, a list of media should come in handy.

Graphic Designers and Printers

Besides using a printer to print your book, printers can print any type of promotional material you can think of. Of course, they can only print what has already been designed; so make sure your piece is designed to be high impact and attention grabbing.

Selecting a graphic designer and printer is like hiring any other professional. You'll want to get referrals from people who have used them, see samples of their work, and get a written estimate and time line. Professionals can only work with what they are given, so you can't assume they know what you want. Come prepared with ideas, colors, pictures, and expectations to work together to create a promotional piece that will help you sell books.

Brian Taylor of Pneuma Books has written an informative case study at the end of this chapter called "Book Design and Beyond." While the article will be of particular interest to self-publishers, those who have published books traditionally will also want to read about what goes into designing the look and feel of a book.

The elements of design that Brian discusses in this case study will be helpful when you either design your own cover or promotional material or hire a professional. The Internet can be of enormous help in searching for a designer, but you can also look closer to home. Printers know designers, so that's one place to start. Asking other authors can lead you to the right designer for you. John Kremer's and Dan Poynter's suppliers lists in the resources section will give you options for both printers and designers.

Media Consultants and Publicists

When it comes to getting radio, television, and print opportunities, it's all about connections. Sometimes it pays to hire a professional in this area. Can most authors create a media kit, send them out, play by the rules, and get results? Of course, they can. The question is: Is that the best use of their time, and is that where they are best gifted?

Media consultants and publicists offer a full range of publicity services, including creating effective promotional materials, crafting media questions, media mailings and follow-up, sending electronic press releases, sometimes coordinating media tours, and generally developing a targeted campaign to get you and your book noticed by both print and electronic media.

As in any business, there are those who do a fantastic job and others who don't. While many of these companies are made up of former publicists with book publishing houses, some are individuals who one day decided they wanted to do this. There is no education or licensing needed to call yourself an expert, so keep that in mind when choosing a publicist or media consultant.

Just as you specialize in the type of writing you do, some publicists also specialize in the services they provide and the type of clients they take on. If a publicist has never coordinated a tour and that is something you want to do, you should probably select someone else. If you are petrified of television and that's a publicist's claim to fame, paying for a service you'll never use makes no sense. If you have a novel and the publicist you're considering has clients who have won the Christy Award and had books on best-seller lists, then you will want to consider hiring her.

You've heard it said that everything is negotiable, and that's the case with this type of service too. After researching a number of firms, you should be able to get a feel for price ranges and services you will need.

Creative Resources, Inc., is a Christian freelance publicity and ministry consulting agency based in Sandpoint, Idaho. "We represent about sixty Christian authors each year and schedule 2,000 radio and television interviews," says Don Otis, co-owner. "We started in Los Angeles in 1991 and have grown every year since. Our mission is "to provide opportunities for communication, growth and development to individuals and organizations by broadening or stimulating public exposure to ideas, resources, and products."

In addition to serving individual clients, he and his wife publish *Media Connections,* an eight-page publication sent send to about 1,000 Christian and secular media. Part of what they do is to help train authors, so they can get the most out of their publicity experiences.

While 90 percent of their clients are Christian publishers like Broadman & Holman, Baker/Revell/Chosen, WaterBrook/Shaw, W Publishing, Zondervan, Promise Press, Youth With a Mission, Nelson, and RiverOak/Cook, Creative Resources also handles authors who choose to hire a publicist themselves.

Many authors want to concentrate on other types of marketing; and not only do they want to get to their next books, they still have families, jobs, church, and other ways to spend the already too-brief twenty-four hours each day. For them, a company like Creative Resources might be the answer to publicity if they can afford the price.

Consultants and publicists are trained to make you and your book look good, and they already have great connections. They are also not going to work for free. Professionals in this area typically charge a monthly or project retainer for their services. There are no guarantees that your book will skyrocket to the top of the best-seller list or that even one book will sell. Most will get you interviews and print opportunities. If your distribution system is working and you give good interviews, you should be able to see some results.

Most book publishers have in-house publicists, and you might be assigned one for a month or two to create a buzz. They might also hire an outside publicist to do the same thing. The publisher will send you an author questionnaire to fill out and return after you sign a contract. The publicist will use your answers to help define the best way to promote your book. The sample questionnaire on my Web site should give you an idea of the type of information you'll need to gather even if you're a self-published author.

Media consultants often have clients who aren't authors, and sometimes they can help create joint opportunities for you. Following this chapter, Amy Smith, owner of Write Ideas, Inc., shares how radio can sell books. Her article, "Putting the Airwaves to Work in Promoting Your Book," will give you ideas and help you understand how a consultant might help. Several media consultants and publicists, who would love to talk with you, are listed in the resource section at the end of this chapter.

Speakers' Bureaus

If you're a speaker, you have a natural way to sell books if you can get speaking engagements. At some point you might want to consider a speakers' bureau to reach those who might be interested in hiring you.

Bureaus make their money by taking a percentage of what you are paid, so they have a great incentive in getting you and other authors as many bookings as possible. Like publicists, speakers' bureaus have spent years building relationships and have gained reputations for having a variety of professional speakers. Churches, women's groups, conferences and conventions, schools, health organizations, and others call bureaus to get speaker recommendations for their events.

A bureau will need one or more examples of talks you have given, preferably in front of an audience; your one sheet; publicity photo; and other material to make an evaluation of whether it can book you. You might be asked to sign an exclusive contract, or you could sign up with several.

Some of the bureaus listed in the resource section may not be taking new clients, while others may require you to go through their training program to be considered. If you'd like a greater selection to choose from, particularly if your primary audience is non-Christian, you might want to contact the National Speakers Association (www.nsaspeaker.org) and ask for a referral.

Web Designers

The last chapter should have made you understand how a Web site can sell books, get speaking engagements, and minister to your readers. This is one area where you don't need to rely on a professional designer if you prefer doing it yourself.

If you do decide to hire a Webmaster, having an idea of what you want is critical in getting a great site. My article on page 171, "Web Design for Authors," includes a list of questions to ask prospective designers, as well as a variety of industry standard design tips you'll want to make sure your designer follows.

My Webmaster husband, Gary, routinely critiques author Web sites and has created a "Ten Point Web Site Evaluation" available for your use. For a copy of the form, go to www.writerspeaker.com/youcan.html.

This chapter contains only an introduction for choosing the right marketing subcontractors. The learning process never ends; and there are newsletters, books, and associations that can help. Both Publishers Marketing Association (PMA) and Small Press Association of North America (SPAN) are good organizations for those who have chosen to self-publish, but the information available on their Web sites or by joining is valuable for anyone with a book to sell.

Cross & Quill from Christian Writers Fellowship International, *The Christian Communicator* and *Advanced Christian Writer* from American Christian Writers, and *WIN-INFORMER* from Writers Information Network are all subscription newsletters/magazines filled with helpful insights on publishing and marketing.

Rather than trying to do everything yourself, I hope you'll explore the possibilities of working with various people who can help you get your message to the world.

Featured Resources

Associations

American Booksellers Association	www.bookweb.org
CBA	www.cbaonline.org
Publishers Marketing Association (PMA)	www.pma-online.org
Small Press Association of North America (SPAN)	www.spannet.org
Writers Guild of America	www.wga.org

Christian Catalog

Christian Book Distributors	www.christianbook.com

Distributors, Fulfillment, Wholesalers

Book Clearing House	www.bookch.com
BookZonePro (extensive list)	www.bookzonepro.com/sources
Dan Poyner's suppliers	www.parapub.com/supplier.cfm?userid=48955711
FaithWorks	www.faithworksonline.com
Ingram Supplier Services	www.Ingrambookgroup.com/pub_info/newpubinfo/issdistributor.htm
John Kremer's suppliers	www.bookmarket.com/databases.html

National Book Network   www.nbnbooks.com
Quality Books
  (library distributor)   www.quality-books.com
Spring Arbor   www.springarbor.com

Designers
Pneuma Books   www.pneumadesign.com/books
Pine Hill Graphics   www.pinehillgraphics.com

Magazines
Christian Retailing   www.Christianretailing.com

Mailing and Catalog Lists
Cahners Mailing Lists   www.cahnerslists.com/lists/index.asp
DecisionMaker Media
  Management   www.dm2lists.com
John Kremer's catalog list   www.bookmarket.com/
    19.html#catalog

John Kremer's marketing   www.bookmarket.com/
  lists (fee)   databases.html

Independent Bookstores
Bookweb's Independent   www.bookweb.org/bookstores/
  Bookstores   browse.html

Media Consultants
The B&B Media Group   www.tbbmedia.com
CMResources Don Otis   www.tbbmedia.com
CLASS   www.CLASServices.com
Creative Resources, Inc.   CMResource@aol.com
DeChant-Hughes
  & Associates   www.dechanthughes.com
Dobson Media Group   www.dobsonmedia.com
Integrated Book Marketing   ibmarket@optonline.net
Jakasa Promotions   jakasajc@bellsouth.net
MediaTalk   www.mediatalk.biz
MRB Consulting   MicheleRBuc@aol.com
Wynn-Wynn Media   wynn@onenet.net

Media Searches
    See pages 77, 110-111

Newsletters and Magazines for Christian Writers
    Advanced Christian Writer   www.ACWriters.com
    The Christian Communicator www.ACWriters.com
    Cross & Quill   www.cwfi-online.org
    WIN-INFORMER   www.bluejaypub.com/win/
                                                  index.htm

Speakers' Bureaus
    Ambassador Agency   www.ambassadoragency.com
    Christian Speakers   www.christianspeakers.com
    CLASS   www.classervices.com
    National Speakers Bureau   www.nsb.com
    Speak Up Speaker Services   www.speakupspeakerservices.com
    Toastmasters   www.toastmasters.org

Book Design and Beyond

by Brian Taylor

Artá Banks has experienced tragedy. Artá discovered her newly adopted child was HIV positive and infected with the AIDS virus. But Artá has also experienced triumph and joy. It is her strength of character and her profound experiences that inspired her to write and publish. Artá wrote a collection of inspirational vignettes. When Artá came to us for copyediting and book design services, we were awed by her testimony. We were also a little concerned about the publishing success she would have. Not because her writing was poor or her stories were boring, but because the type of book she wrote was going to be sold in markets that are already bloated with many titles. Artá's book fit into the inspirational gift market. Like her stories, the book had to be special to compete in the market.

When most writers think of book design, they think of the cover and the title. They think of picking typefaces for the interior, different book sizes and margins, whether to use photos, and other decisions that make a book a book. They get excited thinking about how the book might look sitting in bookstores or how its cover might attract attention.

But book design plays a much more integral role in the success of publishing than you might initially think. In fact, with good planning and execution, book design can open up opportunities to

---

Brian Taylor is the Creative Director of Pneuma Books, the premier book development and marketing solution for publishers. He and his Editorial Director wife, Nina, operate the award-winning company in North East, Md. Their client list includes the Motley Fool Financial Consulting Group, The Foundation Schools, and StreetSmart Books, among many others. Brian is a Mid-Atlantic Publishers' board member and a frequent presenter at writers' conferences. The mission of Pneuma Books is to help writers and publishers succeed by providing education, inspiration, book development, and effective marketing support. They offer a vast Web site devoted to these issues, voted "Best" by InfoSeek. Visit them at www.pneumadesign.com/books.

sell more books in traditional and specialty markets. This was vital for Artá.

Design is making decisions about appearance. But more fundamentally, design is planning and executing. The aspect of design I will focus on here is planning.

Planning Your Course, Directing Your Steps

If you are self-publishing your book, it is strongly recommended that you seek professional assistance in developing, editing, design, and layout. That does not mean you will *not* participate in the design process. Because you will be competing with many other publishers, including the major publishing houses, your book, like Artá's, must be commercially produced. It is imperative for book sales that your book is professional; beautiful; and, above all, commercially developed. It is in the development process that your planning and input will enable the book designer to produce an excellent layout that is appropriate for the marketplace.

I recommended you seek counsel to assist you with your planning. I am speaking of the Holy Spirit. Most likely, God has put it in your heart to write your book. And you are following His directive to do it. You are wisely investing the talents He has given you in order to do it in the best way. However, it is God's. Allow Him to be your co-publisher and employ the professional assistance of the Holy Spirit in your daily activity. Pray about your plan and pray that the Lord gives you wisdom as you execute that plan. And when things become difficult or overwhelming, rely on Him for comfort and reassurance. "In his heart a man plans his course, but the LORD determines his steps" (Proverbs 16:9).

Don't Just Write; Visualize

An excellent design is one that presents the content in the most usable way for the audience. The book designer can create a design that defines your book's persona. But it is up to the author / publisher to plan and write content that can be parceled out by the book designer into heads and subheads; section breaks; sidebars; features; extracts; quotes; and back matter, such as resource appendices, glossary, applications, and samples.

When Artá first came to us for professional assistance with copyediting, design, and layout, her manuscript only contained the collection of stories she had written. Like every manuscript we see, it did need to be copyedited. But we also recommended that she allow us to assist her with some content development.

One of the things we recommended editorially is that Artá include epigraphs to open each story. This was also a part of our design plan. We felt if the chapters opened with a quote for that chapter topic, then we could use that to enhance the overall presentation. This did two things. It made the book look like much more of a gift book—classier and more thoughtful. And, developmentally, it created an opportunity to reach an audience beyond the Christian market. Artá chose epigraphs that were of Ethiopian, Celtic, and Chinese origin; quotes from Thoreau, Lady Bird Johnson, Thomas Jefferson, and Mother Theresa; as well as quotes from her own children, lesser known writers, and even some anonymous sources. This opened up Artá's stories to people from all walks of life.

We also suggested that Artá divide the book thematically into sections. This provided us with the opportunity to create a more luxurious visual presentation with more white space. The result was a more appropriate construction—both developmentally and visually—for the gift book and inspirational/personal growth markets. This revealed the book's purpose.

A Picture's Worth a Thousand Words—or Not

Another tactic we suggested was to select small spot photos for the chapter starts. The task was left to the designer to choose stock photos that communicated the essence of each chapter. This facet of the design capped off a well-rounded visual presentation. With the emotion of the photos, the book became a visual delight and well received in the gift market.

If you plan to use photos, ensure they are the highest commercial quality and that you provide them to the designer in the required format. Poor quality photos, amateur illustrations, and lousy clip art can ruin your professional presentation. Consider whether these additional elements will benefit the content and presentation. If they do not help the reader, do not implement them—that muddies the visual communication. Consider what the impact will be on certain markets. Value adding? Or inappropriate? Many times self-publishers place personal photos or art into their books when it has no real benefit to the content. The result is an amateur presentation that is the stigma of a self-published book. And that ruins your chances in commercial markets. But solid visual elements that genuinely support the topic can add just the right accent.

The point is to consider these things thoroughly. As I stated before, it is up to you to plan these things because a designer might not assist you developmentally in this area—its not his job. His job is to execute a terrific presentation using what you give him. If you give him none of these items because you have not planned well, or you give him poor quality items, or if you give him items without real purpose, then that is what you can expect, regardless of how well the book is designed.

Getting More Support

One more note on additional graphics to support content: Again, consider the value of investing additional development into supporting visuals. If you can produce tables, graphs, diagrams, features, bulleted lists, checklists, examples, exercises that truly support and expound on your subject matter, then you will increase the value of your book in various markets. Your book will be recognized as a better resource by retail, specialty markets, libraries, and academic markets. In addition, consider your own experience when browsing for books in a bookstore. Which one will you select? The one that appears to have only straight text on the subject? Or the one that appears to have quick, handy maps, checklists, diagrams, and tips in support of the content?

It is up to you to consider the implementation of these elements prior to the design and layout stage. It is not a designer's task to recommend these for your content. If you do decide to create this type of a nonfiction book, ensure you provide the content in the appropriate format. If they are tables and charts, make sure they are tab delimited correctly or the costs to reformat the content can skyrocket. If you intend to use diagrams and you have used clip art to develop them, have the designer redo the art in congruence to the design, so the book does not look patched together. Ensure any lists, exercises, forms, etc., are hierarchically correct and well formatted so the layout costs for typesetting are minimized. For more information on this, you can visit our Website section on manuscript preparation and StyleTagging, where there is downloadable information on the process.

A benefit to producing supporting content is that it enables you to repurpose that information for article contribution to magazines, newsletters, Web sites, other books, etc. Those items become marketing tools. If you wish to contribute an excerpt from your book to those publications, the editor will be impressed that you have visuals and will be more likely to accept it. Those elements can also be posted on your book's Web pages or as downloadable resources. They can also be reprinted for target marketing collateral. For instance, if you have a nicely designed chart or diagram that illustrates statistics, it can be used to enhance the message of your subject matter and reinforce the importance of your book to specialty markets.

Pay the Pros to Do What They Do Best, Not to Do Your Work

The developmental assistance we gave Artá Banks did not qualify us for Mensa membership. In fact, most of it was common sense. But it enhanced the overall product. And it helped her look beyond the importance of her own writing for the reader and to the added value for the reading marketplace.

In many cases, when independent publishers contract a copyeditor, the editor simply edits the work for technical issues, such as grammar, usage, spelling, and style. To assist a writer in substantive development exceeds the scope of a copyeditor's contract. Developmental and substantive editing requires more time and more money.

Similarly, many book design and layout firms simply create a good design for the existing content as it is and rarely suggest additional development that would improve the design for specific markets, unless the firm is a full book development firm like ours. But, again, it costs more to do so. Is it worth it? You bet! It is more expensive but yields a better return on your investment. However, you can save money by addressing many of the developmental issues yourself.

The visual characteristics that hallmark your book and improve its market opportunity will come directly from well-developed editorial ideas prior to the execution of the design. A designer is only as good as the content. You can reduce your costs and improve your product if you put more thought and planning into your content prior to contracting professionals.

Getting Results

So how did those decisions play out in Artá's marketing efforts? Direct results are hard to track. However, Artá's book was reviewed personally by the esteemed Jan Nathan, executive director of Publishers Marketing Association, the world's biggest and most active book marketing member organization. In the February 2002 *PMA Newsletter,* she stated:

> This past week, all on one day, three books arrived at my desk which reinforce why I love the world of independent publishing. I think the moon must have been in the seventh house, or something like that.
>
> The first book, *Wrong Feet First* was sent in by a PMA publisher member, Pneuma Books. It was a book in which they played an integral part in the design. And in fact, the design initially attracted me to the book. But then the title, the blurbs on the back, etc. caused me to want more, so I opened it. For the next two hours, I found myself reading the lovely words of Artá Banks. The author, who is not a PMA member, self published the book (her first) and has achieved what many in this world do not. This book could compete with anything currently on the market, not only in design, but also in the writing style and message it delivers. I immediately sent the author an e-mail telling her how much she and the book have enriched my life. This author is new to the world of writing and publishing, but she is a natural at both. No, *Wrong Feet First* is not in every bookstore...

yet. But I am sure one day I am going to be able to say that I remember when I was first introduced to the work of Artá Banks!

Wow. Not bad!

And, praise the Lord, *Wrong Feet First* has won some awards from the Colorado Independent Publishers Awards (The Evvy). It placed third in the category of Inspirational Gift Book and won another third place in the category of Overall Book Design. The aforementioned developmental efforts paid off! But even better, the book won first place in the category of Personal Development.

In addition to the chapter and section development, we recommended to Artá that she create a practical application for the end of each story. These were short questions for contemplation that synthesized the topic of that chapter. We felt if the reader was given a challenge to apply the inspiring material to his or her own life, the book would have more value. We felt it increased its benefits as a gift book, but also improved its chances as a study tool or for use as the focus of discussion groups. The questions were simple: "How is the world different because of you?" "Who's on your team?" and "Is there someone in your life you need to thank?" These questions in combination with the thematic section groupings (such as "Hope," "Family," and "Courage"), the revelation found in the epigraphs, the captivating photos, and Artá's wonderful inspiring stories created a complete personal development tool.

Three awards—more than any other contestant received in this prestigious competition. Winning book awards is an effective marketing tool. It solicits interest from retail, increases publicity opportunities, and extends the shelf life of the book.

The Back Matters

One more note about development. The front and back matter are often overlooked as visual elements. But without these parts, a book is obviously incomplete—and it also *appears* incomplete visually. If a book only contains the sparest of front matter and no back matter, it looks and feels inadequate. As a matter of fact, it is inadequate. If it is a nonfiction work, it should have a proper table of contents and copyright page, as well as a glossary, a proper bibliography, and a proper index. Without these elements, that book will have a slim chance of reaching library, academic, and educational markets.

But well-developed back matter serves much more than the standard book markets. It enables you to sell your book in specialty markets. If you have detailed references and resources on your subject as appendices, then it is likely that each resource you list will carry your book. Furthermore, with well-developed resources, you are enhancing the value of your content.

Artá added resources on adoption and HIV/AIDS organizations. As a result, her book is much more than an inspirational gift book for personal development. It is now a resource. In addition, it is recognized by professionals and laypersons who are close to the subject. Without that small appendix, Artá might have a more difficult time reaching that market base.

Another benefit of this is the ability to repurpose your resource list, bibliography, or glossary as contribution material to those specialty interest areas.

When back matter is well developed, designed, and laid out, books tend to look whole. Another visual dimension is added to the book. Again, it appears more professional and more commercial.

A Campaign Designed around the Design

Once all the components are developed, designed, and laid out, you can use that design as a springboard for all of your marketing materials. You see, a book is a product like any other. It is packaged as a product. The elements that go into the design form the persona of that product's image. That persona must be aligned with the publisher's brand products—other books; books in a series; the publisher philosophy; the publisher's imprint logo; the corporate colors and fonts; the book's images, colors, and fonts. These factors, in combination with the summarized message, or essence, of the book form the foundation of the marketing campaign. The components of the campaign come from the book elements: titles and subtitles, cover images, back-cover copy, interior samples and excerpts, tips and features, and resource lists.

It's All in the Name

Crucial to the success of the campaign is the book cover. The most important aspect is the titling. It is imperative that the title be developed so that it provides effective marketing headlining.

In Artá's book, *Wrong Feet First,* the subtitle is *A Gift of Stories for Your Inside-Out Kind of Day.* Right away the word *gift* is intrinsic in the idea. Its major market is instantly identified. Furthermore, it allows for clever marketing slogans like these:

Having a wrong-feet, inside-out kind of day? Then you should have A Gift of Stories! *Wrong Feet First,* a gift of stories for your inside-out kind of day.

If you've ever had an inside-out kind of day, then put your wrong feet first! *Wrong Feet First,* a gift of delightful stories about hope, family, courage, and dreams to amuse, teach, and inspire.

Even the titles of the sections are used in the marketing copy. Or in deeper copy:

Have you ever had an inside-out kind of day? Artá Banks has had plenty. But Artá has a special gift … the ability to turn those kinds of days right-side up, facing out.

These plays on the title are best produced when the colors, fonts, and images from the cover and the interior are used over and over to hammer home the book identity. This increases brand stability and recognition.

Packaging It All Up

The cover and the interior elements (tips, features, charts, graphs, lists, chapter starts, and other excerpts) should be repurposed for your marketing efforts. I won't detail the specific marketing efforts here because those concepts are discussed in other chapters of this book. I will restate that your efforts should include contributing excerpts of your book to newsletters, Web sites, magazines, e-zines, and so forth. You should also take care to send your book for review to all the book industry venues according to their submission guidelines. And you will need to solicit distributors, retail buyers, and nonretail buyers.

Editors probably won't reproduce your book's design when they run your contribution. But you should still send out your material in a professional package that is congruently designed with your books persona—fonts and layout—and that communicates a campaign derived from the essence of the book, which is ultimately established in the planning and development phases prior to design. This will impress the editors, reviewers, acquisitions librarians, distributors, and retail buyers. It ensures they realize you are a professional. They will clearly understand your book's platform. And, they will take you seriously.

And isn't that what it is all about?

Taking Excellence Seriously

We want our words to be taken seriously. It is important to prepare them thoughtfully and with purpose. And it is important to dress them with professionalism. More importantly, excellence is the key to a successful project. After all, our work is God's plan; and our plan is to do that work with excellence because it is the reflection of Him. So plan, pray, and invest all the talents He gave you in your project. And invest in the talents of those whom God has equipped to help you—the developer, the editor, the designer, and the book marketer.

Looking Backward

At Pneuma Books, we have a method for learning how to plan and develop books. We call it *writing backwards*. It is the process of learning first about what the reading audience expects and desires from a particular book. Secondly, it is the process of understanding the competition and the design/content trends in publishing a particular book and then being able to create a unique but similar approach. Thirdly, it is knowing what the retail and nonretail markets expect, so those markets can be accessed. Fourth, it is establishing a plan to implement the first, second, and third into the content of the book—to develop each part of the book in accordance with the aforementioned guidelines. Lastly is the writing itself. If the writing comes first, it is likely that much of it may have to be retrofitted to accommodate steps one, two, and three. But that's OK; writers are always supposed to rewrite anyway, right?

By following this plan, your book will have success in a variety of markets. And each new market opens up another. I hope this information has been helpful. Thanks for letting me share it with you. Best wishes on your project, and God bless you.

Putting the Airwaves to Work in Promoting Your Book

by Amy Smith

Radio can be a powerful tool in promoting your book. As a media outlet, it has the potential to be targeted in terms of audience and to reach a large number of customers for your book. There are many ways to use radio, and this article will help you target specific stations and shows that are appropriate; design creative promotions to gain awareness for your title; and review case studies of successful book promotions, so you can see which tactics have worked in the past.

Targeting Is Key

Like any marketing exercise, the key is targeting. You need to match the message with the potential receiver of the message in order to achieve maximum impact. One of my favorite books on the subject is *Positioning: The Battle for Your Mind* by Jack Trout and Al Ries (McGraw-Hill). Written by two advertising executives, the book outlines ways to position a message most effectively in a cluttered marketplace such as ours.

So, in radio promotions, you want to evaluate which stations would be the best targets for your book's promotion. Make a list of the stations in the markets you want to target, and list their formats (oldies, adult contemporary, rock 'n roll, easy listening, etc.) and audiences. There are lots of places you can find this information.

The Internet

Most stations have Web sites that list a lot of useful information. Since Web sites are a fairly recent phenomenon for radio,

Amy Smith is Owner of Write Ideas, Inc. (www.writeideas.com), a Maryland-based public relations company that creates and implements more than $4 million in promotions and publicity each year. She is a member of Washington Independent Writers, the Public Relations Society of America, and PRConsultantsGroup.com.

many stations build web-based promotions to drive traffic to their sites. This, too, might be a good place to promote your book. Typically, the contests are promoted on air and executed on site. And many stations have loyal listener clubs, including blast e-mail capabilities that might offer another promotional opportunity.

Media Directories

Media directories are quite expensive ($250 and up), but may be available at a public library, especially one with a business section. Burrelle's and Bacon's are examples with a profile of each station by market. Another good resource is the United Way. In some states, it publishes a local media directory that is available for a nominal fee.

Media Kits

The most comprehensive overview of a station is available in the station's media kit, which is a sales kit to attract advertisers. If you contact the sales department, someone may be willing to send this to you. The key benefit of the media kit is that it lists specific shows and hosts, a great way to target specific programs that make sense for your book title.

The bottom line is that you want to pursue stations that make sense for your book.

Design and Pitch Creative Promotions

With the exception of news-only formats, most radio stations have promotions, such as contests, giveaways, events, and on-air chatter.

These promotions happen in a number of ways. Most frequently, paid advertisers are given radio promotions for free or a fee as part of their advertising packages. There are other avenues, however, such as barter, where products or services are traded for airtime. For example, a health club may donate a year's membership valued at $500 in exchange for $500 worth of airtime. Some smaller stations, or those that have recently changed their format and are trying to attract listeners, may be especially open to barter.

So how can authors take advantage of this marketing opportunity? First, target the right stations. Then, identify the decision maker who can say yes to your proposal. Typically, this is a sales or promotions director. Call the station and ask who is in charge of on-air promotions.

Then present your ideas by phone or in writing. In your pitch, be sure to be flexible, to offer to make sure your promotion is in line with the station's format and promotions guidelines, and to have all prizes in-house prior to the start of the promotion (required by most stations).

Let's discuss the actual pitch and idea creation. Think about your book as a product. It is unique, yet complements a theme. For example, a book on fatherhood would fit well with Father's Day promotions. A book on managing your boss could be promoted on Secretary's Day. A great resource is a book that lists holidays or www.bluemountain.com, which lists all kinds of holidays, some of which might be good timing for creating your promotion.

Think about other products and services that would complement your book, since radio prizes are typically $25-50 and up in terms of value. Your book could be part of a prize package. In listening to the stations that you plan to target, see who else is doing promotions and propose ways you could tie in with existing advertisers. Or approach another business yourself to see if you could create an exciting prize package. For example, a book on nutrition could be packaged with a gift certificate to an organic food store. Make sure the elements fit well together. For example, a Valentine's Day giveaway could include dinner for two, flowers, and a massage, but wouldn't include an oil change.

In your pitch letter, be concise and catchy. You might consider delivering it in a creative way. When my firm was promoting the video release of *Shakespeare in Love* for Blockbuster, we delivered pitch letters with a dozen roses. The letter started, "Let's put romance on your airwaves together."

Finally, mention in your pitch letter how the station's Internet site might offer a promotional opportunity. You might be able to link your Web site, if you have one, to the station's to offer cross-promotions as well.

Case Studies to Increase Your Success

The best way to see what type of promotions is being done is to listen. Through our work with 7-Eleven, we did several local book promotions that are excellent examples of partnering that worked. 7-Eleven used its nationwide network of public relations consultants to do book signings and on-air giveaways to promote these books across the country.

Living Lean

Larry North is a Dallas-based fitness guru, and 7-Eleven is a Dallas-based convenience giant that has introduced a variety of healthy snacks over the past several years. In fact, the chain started a "Nutri-Heaven" section to promote healthy eating. These factors combined made the promotion of North's book a natural. His appearances at 7-Eleven stores were a great way to promote healthy messages and products.

The Working Mom on the Run Manual

7-Eleven, home of "dashboard dining," had several creative marketing campaigns to increase its female customer base. Through innovative product introductions, they wanted to send the message that 7-Eleven had lots to offer the female customer. In promoting this book by Debbie Nigro, the chain underscored that message even further. A working mom on the run is time poor and, therefore, the perfect customer for a convenience store.

Last Call at the 7-Eleven: Fine Dining at 2 a.m., the Search for Spandex People, and Other Reasons to Go on Living

Kevin Cowherd, a writer in Baltimore, Md., published a series of humorous essays, including one on 7-Eleven. The fact that it became a part of the title of his book was a great reason to have book signings and TV interviews at a Baltimore 7-Eleven store.

So, with effective targeting and creative ideas, you, too, can hit the airwaves to increase awareness and sales for your book. Happy writing, and happy promoting!

Marketing to Public Libraries

by Judy Gann

Authors often overlook public libraries as crucial vehicles for getting their books into the hands of those who need them. Yet each year libraries spend over a billion dollars on books and other materials. The mission of public libraries is to provide materials reflecting and meeting the informational and recreational needs of their communities. A balanced library collection includes materials representing the Christian viewpoint, and a large public library system purchases multiple copies of many titles. Schools and public libraries are the major markets for children's books.

Although libraries vary in size and utilize a variety of acquisition procedures, there are general ways to effectively market to public libraries.

Meet Their Standards

In addition to stellar writing, books must have sturdy binding to withstand the repeated use they receive in the public library. Spiral binding is the "kiss of death" for a library book. Spiral-bound books are difficult to shelve and fall apart after only a few circulations.

Make Ordering Easy

Make it as easy as possible for librarians to order your book. Your book should have an ISBN (International Standard Book Number). If you are self-publishing your book, apply for a number through the ISBN Agency, R. R Bowker. A Library of Congress number and Cataloging in Print (CIP) also aid librarians in ordering your book.

Judy Gann is an author and youth services librarian for the Pierce County Library System in Tacoma, Wash. Some of these tips are adapted from *An Author's Guide* by the Collection Management & Youth Services Departments of the Pierce County Library System, Tacoma, Washington, December 1995.

Get Your Book Reviewed

Due to time constraints and the vast number of books published each year, librarians primarily select materials from reviews. Seek to have your book reviewed in the major reviewing journals used by acquisition librarians: *Booklist, Library Journal, School Library Journal,* and *Publishers Weekly.*

Booklist reviews both children and adult materials. Periodically it includes a Christian fiction review column with longer reviews of selected Christian novels. Procedures for submitting titles for review can be found at www.ala.org/booklist/submit.html.

Library Journal reviews adult materials, *School Library Journal* reviews children and young adult materials, and *Publishers Weekly* reviews both children and adult materials.

Some larger library systems also subscribe to *Christian Retailing* and *Christian Library Journal.*

Libraries purchase most of their materials through library wholesalers, which enable them to purchase the majority of materials from one source—a source that provides a deeper discount and greater selection than that offered by publishers. Because wholesalers offer cataloging and processing assistance, libraries save both time and money when purchasing from them. Libraries are more inclined to purchase your book if it is available through their wholesalers.

Major wholesalers serving the library market are Baker & Taylor, Ingram Book Company, and Book Wholesalers, Inc. (only distributes juvenile materials). Spring Arbor Distributors is a division of Ingram.

If your book is self-published and you are your own distributor, use a professional looking invoice, including your business name. However, a library still may prefer to purchase your book through a wholesaler.

Acquaint Them with Your Book

Since libraries don't receive as many review copies of CBA titles as ABA titles, consider sending them review copies of your book.

Avoid faxing, dropping in, or calling when you promote your book. Instead, send a letter introducing your book and yourself. If possible, include a color copy of your book cover, along with any reviews. Libraries increasingly resemble bookstores in the marketing of materials. Today they have more display space for books, rather than strictly shelving them spine out. Therefore, attractive appealing book covers are as important for libraries as bookstores.

Keep in mind libraries' seasons for book ordering. Since January is the beginning of most libraries' budget years, January through March is a key buying period. Most funds must be spent by December, so September through November is another key purchasing time.

Libraries do consider book requests from patrons. They usually look for reviews of requested titles before purchasing though.

Alert local libraries when you've scheduled a book signing or radio interview. They will appreciate the opportunity to be prepared for a possible onslaught of requests for your book.

Librarians realize the quality of Christian books has improved in recent years. Excellent writing that glorifies God and speaks to the heartfelt needs of readers has a place on the shelves of the public library.

Featured Resources

Baker & Taylor, Inc.	www.baker-taylor.com
Book Wholesalers, Inc.	www.bwibooks.com
Booklist	www.ala.org/booklist
R. R. Bowker	www.bowker.com
Christian Library Journal	www.christianlibraryj.org
Christian Retailing	www.christianretailing.com
Ingram Book Company	www.ingrambookgroup.com
Library of Congress	http://cip.loc.gov/cip/
Library Journal	www.libraryjournal.com
Publishers Weekly	http://publishersweekly.reviewsnews.com
School Library Journal	http://slj.reviewsnews.com

Section Four

Executing Your Plan

Chapter **10**

Open House
God-Inspired Author Success Stories

Great men are they who see that spiritual is

stronger than any material force, that thoughts

rule the world.

— Ralph Waldo Emerson

A few years ago I was asked to sing on the worship team for a Christmas Eve service. Several of the regulars were out of town, and they needed a soprano to round out the team.

The church I was attending then had a youthful praise team; and all the female members had long, blond hair and obviously shopped for their very short dresses in the juniors department. If you visit my Web site, you'll see I'm not a blond and my section of the store is not juniors.

My son came to the service, and afterwards I asked him what he thought. "Mom, watching you on the stage made me think of *Sesame Street.*"

Sesame Street? What an odd answer from a 16-year-old boy. He stood in silence, all six-foot-four of him, as I pondered his comment. Finally, I gave in and asked him to explain.

"I don't mean any offense," he started. "But when I saw you up there, all I could think of was that song on *Sesame Street* about one thing not being like others and not belonging."

That might be how you feel about your marketing. You might not have a Web site or be a speaker or have the money to hire a publicist. Don't worry. There are many ideas you will be able to implement and will be perfect for you and your own book. Revel in your uniqueness and that you sometimes feel like you don't belong. It means you're normal and God can use you to reach other people who feel like they don't fit.

This chapter is filled with ideas and stories about authors who probably didn't "fit" at some point in their marketing. I invite you to read, learn, and add any of these to your toolbox. You'll want to tweak them and make them right for you, but there's something for everyone. I hope you enjoy these God-inspired success stories.

Articles

Suzanne Eller published hundreds of articles before the release of her book, *Real Teens, Real Stories, Real Life* (RiverOak); and now she's writing articles as part of her book promotion. "I've written Web e-zine articles to promote my books," explains Suzanne. However, promotion is only the secondary reason while ministry is the first. "My column on CBN.org is a great way to minister to teens."

Joan Esherick's book, *Our Mighty Fortress* (Moody) was featured in the "New and Noteworthy" book review section of *Moody*. That alone would be a thrill, but there was something else in that issue. "I had a feature article on prioritizing/decision making ("Good, Better, Best"), and the byline listed me as the author of *Our Mighty Fortress*. It was a really nice tie in."

Cherry Pedrick, R.N., wrote articles for magazines just before New Harbinger published her first book, *The OCD Workbook*. "I had to swallow my pride when a national women's magazine wanted to publish my story, but as an "as told to" story. The byline went to another writer, but my book still received valuable publicity.

Cherry also writes for Suite101, an Internet portal where she gains exposure for all her books. She writes on the subjects of obsessive-compulsive disorder and habits to help educate people about the subjects. "The columns were well-established when the books were published. Links to my book Web sites were listed prominently."

Author on Board

March 12, six months and a day after the September 11 attacks, Dianne Butts picked up her new book, *Dear America: A Letter of Comfort and Hope to a Grieving Nation* (Ampelos Press). She sent newsletters to her Christmas list and set up book signings in the small towns where she has lived, but these efforts were only reaching the people she knows. She knew she would have to try something new and creative to reach people outside her circle of friends.

Dianne rides a motorcycle and came up with a fun way to promote her book:

> The day before my husband and I were scheduled to take a four-day trip, I had an idea. I used my computer to make a diamond-shaped sign that reads "Author on Board." I printed it on the brightest yellow paper I could find and then laminated it. I found a folder that my sign would fit in and not get crushed on my motorcycle, tucked in some flyers with order forms, loaded my traveling box with copies of my book, found an extra bungee cord, and stuffed it all in the pack on my bike.
>
> On our trip, every time we stopped for any length of time, whether for a meal at a restaurant or a hotel to spend the night, I stretched the bungee cord across my windshield, slid my "Author on Board" sign under the bungee, and tucked a few flyers in beside it."

Her sign attracted some attention, and she ended up selling five books that short weekend. "When I travel in the car, instead of using the bungee cord, I tuck the sign and flyers under the windshield wiper. When I am genuinely interested in the people around me who cross my path, they are interested in me and my book. It takes time out of my busy writing schedule to talk to people. But it often brings the greatest rewards. And I'm not just talking book sales!"

Autographed Copy Stickers

Kristy Dykes does book signings, and presigns her books for speaking engagements. She places gold metallic "Autographed Copy" stickers on each one. If people want her to, she graciously signs the recipient's name to add a personalized touch.

Kristy also believes in the power of promotion. "With a degree in mass communications/journalism, I had to take PR courses; so I know the importance of it. Also, I have lived a life of "friend raising," being interested in others, so now they are interested in me. I believe in shameless self-promotion (in a tasteful, God-pleasing way). If we know that God has gifted us with talents, we should be proud of them (in a good way) and seek to use them for His glory.

Bookmarks

Children's author Verla Kay designs and uses creative bookmarks that list her available books on the front, along with her contact information. "Try to put something on the backs of them that will make people want to keep them. A fun game, a quiz pertaining to something in your books, or facts they will want to remember are some things you can use. Give them out freely! Pass them out to children and teachers during school visits, put them out on the freebie tables when you attend conferences, slip them into your books when you visit bookstores."

Book Club (Reading Club)

Lauraine Snelling is the award-winning author of over forty novels for both adults and young adults. Her book *The Healing Quilt* (WaterBrook) is an excellent choice for a beginning book club because it lends itself well to discussion. She encourages bookstores to host a club because it will increase traffic; but a home, church, restaurant, or library meeting room can work well for a location. She gives stores these suggestions: "Several months before beginning, post a sign-up list at your store, including phone numbers. Talk it up, get your employees excited about it. Encourage people to sign up. Publicize it through your store newsletter."

So who makes a good contact? Anyone who loves to read and talk about books. The contact chooses the book for the first discussion. Hopefully that person will choose one of your books if you are the one suggesting a club. The host needs to decide up front if the club will be a fiction, nonfiction, or mixed genre club. If the host doesn't know what to start with, then bookstore employees or readers can recommend titles.

Of course, a book club needs promotion, which is the next step. Lauraine suggests these ideas for bookstores: "Get a poster from the publisher or make one; and set the book on a counter with a sign that says this is the first book to be read for the book club. Order plenty of books, more than the number who have signed up since some will buy the book just because you have it set out in front like that. Have the books in the store a month before the first meeting. Phone people to remind them the book is in, so they can come in and purchase it."

Now comes the fun part. The day of the meeting, Lauraine recommends having someone from the store staff moderate unless there's a volunteer from one of the customers. Here are a few other tips for that first time: "Provide beverages, snacks, and discussion questions to start with. Some books already have discussion questions available. Sometimes you can get these by calling the publisher or contacting the author via her Web site. Make sure you have enough chairs. Also have a list of possible books for the group to choose from."

The group votes at this meeting on what they will read and discuss at the next several meetings, so you can publicize and order the books. The goal is for the group to become self-sustaining and have a great time together. Some books lend themselves more to discussions than others, so thought-provoking questions are good. If someone doesn't like the book, that's the way life is.

Some stores have more than one book club, depending on what the groups want. Besides fiction or nonfiction, there can be children's groups too.

Lauraine continues her suggestions for stores: "Word of mouth will build the group, but in-store publicity is important. The group will become as important as you think it is. Some stores have even been forced to keep the book club books behind the counter, so members can get their copies. Now isn't that a great problem?"

If you use one of her books and you notify her, Lauraine will send bookmarks and discussion questions for that title.

ReadingGroupGuides.com is a site devoted to book clubs and reading guides. Visit this site to see if it will list your book and guidelines. Be sure to check out its sister sites, Authors on the Web, Teens Read, and Kids Read.

Bookplates

Bookplates can also be a fun item to give away or affix to books donated to libraries, hospitals, and schools. Your Web site or a toll-free number can be added to let people know how to order your book.

A quick search on the Internet will reveal an impressive number of companies offering custom designed or standard bookplates for sale. With a color printer and the right supplies, you can design your own bookplates too. Children's author Anne Fine offers free ones on her site.

Book Signings

Caron Loveless is not particularly sold on the overall productivity of book signings, but each year the largest Barnes and Noble store in her area invites regional authors with new books to do a half-day book signing. When she heard about this, she jumped at the chance to participate since she figured it might be the only opportunity she'd ever get to sign books in a Barnes and Noble.

The day of the signing I was ushered upstairs with about eight other authors and given my own table with a stack of two of my book titles, which the store had preordered. I brought with me an extra-large, laminated mockup of my latest book cover—which I displayed—and more business cards than the average realtor hands out in a month.

At first I was worried that so many authors in one place would lessen my opportunity for sales. But it didn't take long for me to learn that one of the great things about a group signing is that you don't have to stand there alone praying for someone to ask directions to the rest room. I discovered that there's strength in numbers; and while you're eagerly waiting for customers, it's fun getting to know the other authors and hearing about their work.

This particular day was a good one for me. I sold out of all the books on my table, in part due to the fact that I had cleverly announced to my friends and neighbors that I would be doing a Barnes and Noble book signing and could use their moral support. Apparently my sell out caught the attention of the store buyer who promptly ordered more of my books. I assume that's the reason why, on a certain day that next week, Amazon.com noted that my book, *The Words That Inspired the Dreams* (Howard), was the number one best-selling book in Orlando, Fla.

Caron didn't stop there. When one of her neighbors dropped by her Barnes and Noble book signing, she made a point of asking another author to snap their picture together with her book cover face out, of course. A few days later, she mailed the photo, along with pertinent information, to one of the largest news magazines in her area. Within a few weeks, the photo ran in the magazine, which is mailed free to thousands of homes, with a caption and brief write-up, which naturally included the name of her book.

Courting the Media

When Neva Andrews, author of the Jo Barkley Books including *Wild Horse Summer* (iUniverse), got her first books, she dropped into the newspaper office in a nearby small town to leave a review copy. The editor interviewed her on the spot. Ah, the beauty of living in a small town.

Neva explains: "Next week's paper carried a front-page story, complete with picture, big hat and all. The local gift shop invited me to have a book signing. The English as a Foreign Language (ESL) teacher from the local junior/senior high school dropped in. He hadn't even seen the advertising. He looked the book over carefully and said, 'I think this is just what I've been looking for.' He wanted something with content that his students could handle. (*Wild Horse Summer* is a fourth grade reading level.)"

Before Neva knew it, the small town machine kicked into gear and a reporter with the *Greeley Tribune,* the big paper in her part of Weld County, Colo., and a photographer interviewed her. "She wrote a wonderful feature story about me and my books and the way these 14- to 17-year-olds had related to my 10-year-old character. Most of the students are Spanish speakers, but a few were from Japan; and a copy of the book went home with each of them.

Donations

Joan Esherick has donated her book to be used as a door prize or giveaway at conferences (writer's conferences, women's ministry forums, retreats, etc.). "That's generated some interest, particularly if I was only one of several seminar presenters and had a sales table at the conference. By seeing the book as a giveaway, people who otherwise would not have noticed my table or who did not attend my seminars had the opportunity to be made aware of it."

Fan Clubs

Janet and Stephen Bly are big believers in fan clubs. They call theirs the Bly Book Discussion Group. "It was initiated by a woman who has met us and read lots of our books and asked us about doing it," Janet explains. "She set it up on Yahoo and is the moderator. My husband and I are the co-moderators and enter into the discussion whenever it seems appropriate, but mostly the members chat among themselves in e-mail format. We send the moderator potential names when fans write to us and include their addresses. Also, sign-ups happen because of a link on our Web site. It's been a wonderful way for us to discuss details about ourselves and our books and to provide other information that only these participants know. It's very interactive, and they talk about other authors and their books, too, which we don't mind a bit."

Festivals and Trade Shows

Who says a self-published fiction book can't get shelf space or win awards? Christy Award winner, Rosey Dow knew her book *Reaping the Whirlwind* (WinePress) was a winner; and now everyone else does too.

Rosey's novel is a mystery based on the Scopes trial. Through her contact with a Scopes trial expert, she received an invitation to attend the 75th Anniversary Scopes Trial Festival in Dayton, Tenn. Besides selling books, Rosey made key contacts, including the producer of a movie about the Scopes trial who is keeping her name in the event they need an expert down the road.

Not one to miss an opportunity, Rosey went to the CBA convention on the way to Tennessee. She worked the floor, did book signings and media interviews, and made sure people knew about her book.

Obviously excellent writing and awareness paid off. If you visit Rosey's Web site, you can see her 2001 Christy Award sticker.

Giveaways

Jan Coleman, of "Locust Licks" fame, bought lollipops that have wide, flat fronts. She made labels printed with her book title (like the locust licks) and brought them to her book signing to hand out to passerby. She also printed Grasshopper Pie recipes on three-inch by five-inch card stock with book information on the back. She hands them out everywhere. People are likely to keep the dessert recipe for a while. She also sends them out with all her thank-you notes after radio interviews.

Before Wilburta Arrowood's first book, *For the Love of a Child* (Publishing Designs), is released, she's getting ready to promote it. She is collecting butterfly items that go with her ministry theme based on a quote from Nathaniel Hawthorne:

> I visited a store where I found the neatest enameled butterfly bookmarks at a very reasonable price. Since my unofficial logo is a butterfly, I bought almost one hundred of them (all they had) to use as a promo piece when I hand sell my books.
>
> My daughter has made a beautiful plastic canvas basket with butterflies all around it, and I plan to use it as a collection "box" for entries in an in-store contest at my signings. The contest will be open to anyone in the store, not just book purchasers. Prizes will be small—chocolates, cologne, maybe a large box of tissues in a pretty plastic canvas dispenser— something for a fun way to collect e-mail and snail mail addresses for my mailing list.

Wilburta also bought a stamp set to create an unusual marketing too. She plans on stamping her name and Web site address into some Play-Doh® modeling compound. Then she'll pour a plaster of paris mold of it, turn it out when dry, and take it to the dental office where she works. The dentist has agreed to let her use their sterile "suck down plastic" to make a mold of it. (This is what is used to make soft mouth guards.) When it is completed, Wilburta intends to use the molds to make custom chocolates to hand out as a promotional piece. Sweet!

Gonzo Marketing

"When my third book, *Oxygen* (Bethany), came out, my coauthor and I decided to do something wild and crazy," explains best-selling author Randy Ingermanson:

> *Oxygen* is a novel—think *Apollo 13* on the way to Mars and you've got the story line. My coauthor, John Olson, is known for his extremely elaborate parties. We decided to have an *Oxygen* party at John's house in the San Francisco Bay Area.
>
> We invited the world—or close to it. John sent invitations to about 150 people, hoping for half of them to show up. They did. He created descriptions of eight different alien races. He

also made up some human categories—journalists, astronauts, etc. Everybody who came to the party was assigned to either an alien race or a human category. He gave each person a sheet of paper with their goals for the party and points assigned to each goal. One of the lucky attendees was assigned the task of murdering me.

So halfway through the party, I was shot dead with a starter pistol in a secluded part of the house. The party then turned into a murder mystery, with extra points for whoever found my murderer. I floated around for the rest of the party as a ghost, wrapped in a sheet and looking very stupid.

One more wrinkle. Randy and John invited some newspaper people. They wound up with long articles and photos in three different Bay Area newspapers. One of those has a circulation of over a million, and the article wound up on the Web.

Randy continues: "At the end of the party, we sold and autographed books and ate the cake that was decorated with a picture of the cover of our book. Did we make money on this scheme? Not really. Did we have fun? Yes. Did we get way more free advertising than we ever thought possible? You better believe it. Would we do it again? We're still recovering from the last one, but we're thinking about it. This time, John needs to get murdered. I've already donated my body once to the cause."

Have Book, Will Travel

Speakers who travel will have no trouble doing what Eva Marie Everson suggests to create awareness about her books, *Shadow of Dreams* and *Summon the Shadows* (Barbour). "Don't forget to always carry two or three copies of your latest title with you on the plane," she suggests. The conversation sounds something like this:

"And what do you do?"

"I'm an author."

"Really? What do you write?"

"Books!" Then Eva Marie whips out a copy. If people tell her they like this kind of book, she signs it to them. If she has the opportunity to chat with the flight attendants, she asks them what they like to read. If their tastes match her books, they get a copy too. Imagine how many potential readers seat mates and flight attendants can tell about your book in airports alone.

Join, Join, Join

Janet and Ron Benry write mystery and suspense, and they have found joining several organizations that support writers of this genre has been helpful in selling their titles. "We both belong to Sisters-in-Crime, and attend (not as often as we'd like) local chapter meetings. We've been asked to speak at these luncheons. This is a good venue for us because the Sisters (men can be sisters) buy and write mysteries. Ron has joined Mystery Writers of America and is trying to get local chapter members together for a meeting, something that hasn't been done."

Janet is on the DorothyL e-mail list (Dorothy L. Sayers). The list discusses mysteries, plus a good number of the members are librarians and fans of mystery. Both Ron and Jan belong to Murder Must Advertise, a Yahoo mystery group. By being involved in this group, they get their names out to people who write mysteries.

Janet explains, "Writers of mysteries are readers of mysteries and, therefore, buyers of mystery books. The fact that we write Christian books doesn't seem to be a problem, although I'm sure some will not buy them for that reason. But then, others will and have."

As Janet says, "So, what's the theme here? Join, join, join."

Marketing Purses

Allison Bottke, creator and editor of God Allows U-Turns (Barbour) came up with a fabulous idea. Sorry guys, this is one of those "ladies only" strategies, though she gives credit for the idea to her husband. "My sweet husband had a purse made for me using the covers of volumes one and two of God Allows U-Turns. He is a real estate broker who sold a home to a lady who makes these purses for a living. However, she does not do custom work. Her clients are all over the world and she mainly makes Rolling Stone magazines and old record album covers into purses and ships them to countless gift and specialty houses."

Allison explains how much fun it was to carry her book at the CBA convention last summer. When she decided to take her purse, she contacted this purse designer and asked her if she would be willing to make custom purses as a special favor for some fellow authors. She had a purse made for her friend, Eva Marie Everson, to carry around CBA boldly marketing her two suspense novels.

The attention-grabbing purses can be filled with postcards and other promotional pieces. Allison says they are $100 each, which is rather expensive; but you probably will have a tough time finding a more fun or unique marketing idea.

Newsletters

Newsletters, whether sent via snail mail or electronically, can be a great way of keeping in touch with readers and, hopefully, selling more books.

Jim Watkins, author and director of the Sandy Cove Christian Communicators Conference, has a fun electronic newsletter called *SPAM of the Month Club,* featuring his best newspaper column for that month. Jim gives visitors a reason to sign up for his newsletter since subscribers get access to the exclusive SPAM of the Month site, featuring Jim's favorite reference sites.

More and more authors have newsletters. Consider visiting publishers' Web sites to see if some of their best-selling authors have a newsletter or Web site. By seeing what successful authors are doing to promote their books, you can get lots of ideas.

Don't forget to send out notices that might appear in other people's newsletters. Cherry Pedrick says, "For all my books, I've sent notices that were published in my nursing school alumni newsletter."

Nursing Homes

Lucy L. Woodward is the co-author of an inspirational book for seniors titled *Gift of Years.* Her book is a collection of lasting messages of love, joy, and promise aimed at older people. The book was published by Ark Books, which later sold out to a publisher that went bankrupt. Lucy and her co-author, Margaret Wyatt, worried that the remaining inventory would be remaindered and possibly disposed of. With the help of Dave Stuart Ministries in California, they were able to obtain all remaining copies of the second printing of 5,000 at cost. Lucy reports:

> Periodically I have contacted nursing homes and assisted living homes, offering to visit and read poetry and meditations from the book. Because they are more alert and many can still read, people who live in assisted living homes are more interested than patients in nursing homes. I have had a pleasant and rewarding time sharing these helpful and comforting poems with the older folks. Often they will want to buy and keep a copy for themselves, or a relative will buy one as a gift. Word spreads to relatives, and I receive letters and requests

from senior citizens all over the country. I've enjoyed using *Gift of Years* as a ministry in this way. I also leave sample copies containing my address and phone number in local doctor's offices. Patients wanting to buy a copy will call me.

Parades

Traci DePree and her family live in Minnesota in the land of the Jolly Green Giant. Each year the town has a "Giant Days" celebration—named for the big green guy. Four or five thousand people turn out for the parade, so Traci decided to get involved. "My husband and the local Friends of the Library created a float. The theme was "Get Caught Reading" with little scenes—a couple of couches back to back with readers reclining as they read, a man in a bathtub complete with bubble machine, me behind a desk with a typewriter and a dictionary, and on the back a fishing dock with kids holding rods with books tied to the ends. It was a big hit. The crowd literally broke into applause when they saw us, although I think it might have had a lot to do with the man in the tub! Jeff is a really good sport; he took it in stride. It was great fun."

It was more than just fun. They passed out almost 2,000 postcards with a picture of the cover of her newest book, *A Can of Peas* (WaterBrook), and an announcement about the book signing in the park after the parade. "At the signing I sold over 120 books in only three hours! I was signing constantly; my hand still hurts! All in all it was a big success. There are a lot of books out there that weren't there before; and many of them were sold to people from out of town, so the book is gathering legs. The Corner Drug Store in LeSueur sold almost 150 copies in the first two weeks that the book was out and had to order more for a waiting list! Can you tell I'm excited?"

There must be something about small town drugstores. According to Traci another one is now selling her book. "The local drugstore wanted to do a signing. The owner set me up just inside the door and had a manicurist set up at another table. Refreshments—free flavored coffee and buttermilk smoothies that were delicious—were served, and a flutist played the whole while. It was a lovely getaway for all who entered the store!"

Picture Business Cards

At the last CBA convention, I noticed that several authors, including Janet Holm McHenry and Wendy Lawton, had business cards anyone can make using card stock and a color inkjet printer. Janet's business card featured the cover of *Prayer Walk* (WaterBrook), while Wendy's two new releases, *Courage to Run* and *The Tinker's Daughter* (Moody) graced her card.

The publishers created the cards for their authors, but this is one idea that anyone can do.

Possible Dreams: Wal-Mart

To flight attendant Marsha Marks nothing is impossible, including getting her book into Wal-Mart®, a market most major publishers can't crack. "I had this new book, *101 Amazing Things About God* (RiverOak) out in October 2001 and no way for anyone in my little town to buy it. The nearest bookstore was almost an hour drive away, and the only thing for miles around was a Wal-Mart®. So I wanted my book there."

Marsha suspected if it sold well in that store, the other 3,000 stores might carry it as well. She had no idea how to get the chain to carry it, but she knew it would have to be something that started at a grass roots level. "I made a huge mistake in the beginning by going into the Wal-Mart® around here and simply speaking to the manager of the book department. Don't do that. Your request goes nowhere and makes everyone mad. Then I learned to go directly to the store manager. Then I learned the real trick. I gave the book away to a couple of local working women who were the assertive type. And I told them to please go into the local Wal-Mart®, ask to speak to the general manager, and say, 'We want you to carry this book! All our friends want to buy it!' I gave the women a brochure about the book, which listed the title, a picture of it, the ISBN, and the publisher."

Marsha also left the same brochure with the general manager, but she didn't stop there. Whenever she had a signing anywhere in the state, she took the brochure from the signings to the managers of Wal-Mart® stores and showed them the sales figures. She sold an average of one hundred books at signings in Barnes and Nobles, Borders, and other chains.

Things started coming together when Marsha was offered a 500-word column in the tiny weekly paper in her town, which has a circulation of maybe 3,000. "At the end of my column, for which I was paid $15 a week, I advertised my book. Then I gave copies of the column to local people and asked them to take it into Wal-Mart®, ask for the general manager, leave the column with that person, and tell him or her they wanted me in for a signing."

As she puts it, her "pummel marketing" by the locals about her book paid off after about a month. "I got a call from the general manager of our local Wal-Mart® who wanted to book me for a signing. He said, 'We've never had a book-signing here before, but the community wants one, and we are community driven.' I made sure there was plenty of advertising for that signing, and it was before Christmas."

She sold 150 books during the three hours she was in the store. After that, she did two more signings for the local Wal-Mart®, never selling less than 75 books. "I did this by just inviting people who were in the store to read one chapter of my book for free, while they were in the store. And by lots of advertising over the P.A system. By now I was working with the local Anderson Marketing reps who supplied the stores. It's important to work with the suppliers to the stores, once the manager requests the signings. You can go into Wal-Mart® and find out what days the Anderson suppliers are in the stores and become their new best friend and tell them about your book. But that will do nothing if the public isn't requesting that the store manager carry the book, as well."

After three successful signings, Wal-Mart® turned Marsha over to their corporate distributor, Anderson Merchandising. Someone in the corporate office contacted her, and she did more signings.

Marsha gives much of her Wal-Mart® success to that tiny weekly column. "In our little community, in the deep South, everyone goes to church; and my book is about the Bible and its relationship to our lives. My column is the same type of writing as my book. So, I had a built-in support staff of community advocates helping me get my book in Wal-Mart®. Once you are successful in one store, word spreads. Or in my case, I spread it myself—to more local advocates. For instance, when I would visit my in-laws in Lincoln, Neb., I'd speak at local churches, give brochures to people, select one or two assertive types from the crowd, and ask them to go into the local Wal-Mart® and ask for the general manager and request they order this book. In this way, I got my little publicity/sales force going. And got invited to sign at Wal-Mart® stores in other states."

101 Amazing Things About God sold more than 20,000 copies in the first six months.

While having the book in Wal-Mart® didn't hurt, Marsha ensured her success by contacting Choice Books. Choice is a huge distributor that services 600 stores with rack sales. She found the Choice Web site and sent an e-mail telling about her book and asking them to carry it.

"They decided to try it. About a month later, I got an e-mail back thanking me for suggesting my book to them and telling me they had tested it and it sold well. So they were now going to be ordering it for more of their stores."

Marsha hasn't quit her day job as a flight attendant, so she still frequents airport bookstores where her book is available thanks to Choice. Is God good or what?

Presents—Partnering with Your Publisher

Funny lady Laura Jensen Walker has come a long way since her first book, *Dated Jekyll, Married Hyde* (Bethany), was published. As a new author she was looking for ways to become a marketing partner with her publisher, so she was thrilled when she heard from an editor at a conference what one of his authors had done for book promotion. The editor's story got Laura's creative juices flowing, and she came up with an idea for "wedding gifts" for the Bethany sales reps.

She went to several party supply and craft stores and bought little things that related to some of the book's chapters, such as Soap-on-a-Rope for "Calgon vs. Soap-on-a-Rope," a compass for "Directionally Impaired," a red votive candle for "The Night He Saw Red," etc. After her shopping spree the work began for Laura and her husband:

> Michael and I bought pretty wedding wrapping paper, ribbon, wedding confetti, etc., and wrapped each item individually. With the soap I included a small packet of Oreo® cookies and a tea bag because I tell the story of liking to have tea and cookies in the bath sometimes. And for the "Nightmare on Our Street" chapter—about buying our first home—where I talked about the hideous wallpaper in our kitchen, I wrapped and sent bits of the ugly wallpaper. We attached little tags to each "gift" with the chapter title on it, and put all of the gifts in a small mailing box with the pretty wedding confetti sprinkled in. Plus I wrote a fun letter to the sales reps thanking them for selling my first book and expressing my enthusiasm and excitement about it. I signed it, "Profitably yours? Laura Jensen Walker" and mailed the packages to the twenty sales reps.

Laura remembers it cost about $250 for everything, including postage, but it was money well spent. "Needless to say, the reps were delighted and impressed; and, as a result, I suggested we partner together to send packages to some of the top accounts when the book released. I'd be happy to do all the grunt work of assembling the packages if they could pay for it. And they did! I can't remember the exact number now, but I think it was around 50 packages (we included only three items, rather than the six or seven we'd done for the sales reps—no wallpaper this time since we'd run out). We set up an assembly line in my office. My mom, step dad, sister, Michael, and I put all the boxes together, along with a copy of the hot-off-the-presses book and a letter from Bethany to their top 50-or-so accounts (including their chain store buyers)."

Laura took her idea with her when she signed a contract with Revell. The publisher was going to a sales conference with her book, *Thanks for the Mammogram,* and she thought long and hard about what gifts to send about a book on breast cancer. "Finally, I decided the safest—and most tasteful thing to do—would be to bake them sugar cookies, frost them white, and 'write' the pink breast cancer ribbon on top in pink frosting. I overnighted them for freshness, again including a letter thanking them so much for publishing my heart book, for wanting to help women going through cancer, and telling them how much it meant to me. That made a lasting impression because more than two years later at this past CBA, the president of the company—Dwight Baker—mentioned those cookies to me."

QVC

In February 2001, Gail Hayes started writing an online devotion for women. A month after starting her devotional, a woman contacted her via e-mail and said that the messages were a great blessing to her and several other women and that she had shared them during a work place Bible study. When Gail asked if she could use the woman's comments to let others know about the devotions, the woman suggested she call Gail.

"She called; and during the course of our conversation, she told me that she believed that she was to help me. I had no idea who she was or how she could help. She then told me that she was the executive assistant to the vice president of public relations for QVC and she wanted me to send her a promotional package, along with a copy of *Daughters of the King* (Joshua Publishing) and any other items I felt were appropriate."

First Gail thought she was joking since she didn't know that QVC had an inspirational line of products. Within twenty-four hours of receiving Gail's package, that woman set up a telephone meeting with a buyer. By the first week of May, the book had been approved as a new QVC product. It would have been earlier, but Gail also has a set of bookmarks that accompany the book that had to be redesigned to meet QVC specifications.

August 30, 2001, Gail appeared on QVC and sold the set—the book and accompanying bookmarks. So why Gail and her book? "First of all, it is unique. I sold the book and its unique concept to the buyer during our telephone meeting. I felt confident in my product and told him why. I was prepared for that moment in time."

Gail has not stopped creating opportunities for her or her book. "Through making a call and introducing myself to the producer, I landed on the national television network Total Christian Television, which reaches over 40 million homes in the United States and Canada. The day I called, the producer had just had a guest cancel. He immediately booked me as a replacement! I also called a friend, whom I had not spoken with for over a year, and she immediately scheduled a meeting with a representative from the Trinity Broadcasting Network."

Relationship Reviews

A few months after its release, I began getting e-mail messages and letters from members of the Huntington's community who loved *Faces of Huntington's*. When one of these notes came in from an individual with a large circle of influence, I asked them for a favor: Would they send a letter, on their letterhead, to anyone they knew who would benefit from reading my book? I crafted a letter, based on their comments, and e-mailed it to them. Using their letterhead, several doctors, social workers, and researchers graciously used what I wrote and added their signatures and titles. They sent praises for my book to potential buyers from major hospitals and medical schools. Their five-star reviews resulted in direct sales from people I had no easy way of reaching; and some of these were bulk sales, which was even better.

Reading Conferences

Verla Kay, author of *Broken Feather* (Putnam), believes in attending as many reading conferences as possible. She suggests you offer to be a speaker and talk about something teachers can take back and use in their classrooms:

How to get children excited about books, about writing, teaching children how to write, etc., are all good topics. If your books have any school curriculum connections at all, capitalize on that relationship. A session on bringing history or science or math alive in the classroom, using both your books and many others, is a great way to become a speaker at these conferences. When teachers and educators come to your sessions, they will notice your books. If your books are good, they will buy them. And they will tell other teachers.

Many educators attend these conferences looking for authors to bring to their schools for visits. When you do school visits, the children and teachers become familiar with your books, and you can augment your income with speaker fees. Many authors make more off their speaking engagements than they do from their books!

According to Verla, some schools sell hundreds of books during these events; others don't sell any. But even if they don't sell a single book, your name has become bigger and more familiar to everyone in that school. And it's the author's name that sells books.

Retail Outlets (nonbookstores)

Brenda Nixon believes in the "ask and you shall receive" process of selling books. On a recent family trip from Ohio to Idaho where her husband's family lives, she was determined to market her books to unusual outlets. One day they stopped in the tiny southern Idaho town of Montpelier.

"After snapping a few pictures," Brenda shares, "we strolled into the local pharmacy to stretch our legs and cool off. I noticed a young woman behind the cash register with a baby on one hip and two youngsters clinging to her legs. Gift items and books neatly lined the glass display shelves.

"'Do you have a lot of young families here?' I asked the gal. 'Oh yes!' she answered. So I showed my book, *Parenting Power in the Early Years*, to her. I asked if the store might want to stock some for their customers. She explained that her husband was the pharmacist and together they ran the business. On the spot, she purchased six copies of my book to retail at the Montpelier store."

Gary Stanley, author of *What My Dog Has Taught Me About Life* (Honor), has his wife, Luci, to thank for this marketing tip. She was at the beauty salon one day and noticed that the customers were reading various magazines and thought her husband's book of short stories would make great reading material for those under the dryer. Luci gave the shop a copy of the book; as folks started to read it, they began to ask where they could get copies of their own.

Luci's hairstylist finally called and asked if they could supply some copies. As the Christmas season approached, Gary autographed copies that dozens of customer bought. "Because of her business license, she could easily sell them at the store and split the profits with us. We've since done the same thing with my latest book, *How to Make a Moose Run and Other Great Things My Dad Taught Me* (RiverOak)."

The couple also discovered a local distributor that supplies most of the gift stores. Gary and Luci took them a box of dog and moose books, and the distributor took them to a local show. As a result, they now have signed with the distributor, which has a sales force to help get it into more nonbookstore retail outlets. "I think what we've really learned is that I'm much better at writing books, and Luci is much better at finding ways to market them," Gary says.

Singing Your Book's Praises

Laura Jensen Walker, author of *Through the Rocky Road and into the Rainbow Sherbet: Hope & Laughter for Life's Hard Licks* (Revell) is filled with unique ideas for promoting a book. While this idea is about her first book, I'm sure she's thought of some great fun for a book about ice cream. Can you say Ben and Jerry's?

Near the end of the year, when my radio interviews and sales had slowed down a bit, I came up with the idea to send out a fun letter to radio and TV stations in advance of Valentine's Day. I wrote a song parody to the tune of "Love and Marriage"; but I said, "Dated Jekyll, married Hyde." I partnered with Bethany's publicity department. It was my idea, and I wrote the letter; but they printed it on fun stationary and mailed it to a mass of radio and TV stations. And guess what? I got a new rash of radio interviews—and an appearance on *The 700 Club!* The latter wasn't strictly due to the letter; the Bethany publicist has a good and long-standing reputation with all media, and I'm sure that helped a bit. But I didn't get the request to appear until after we'd sent out the mailing six months after the book released. My publicist was pleased because, at the time, she said they hardly ever had their authors get on *The 700 Club*. So everyone was happy all around.

School Ties

Dr. Harry Kraus writes medical mysteries; his most recent book is *Could I Have This Dance?* (Zondervan). He has one easy suggestion about marketing your book: "Don't forget to fill out those annoying alumni update cards from all the institutions where you studied. Add a few lines about your newest book, and it will show up in the latest alumni news publication mailed to other alumni at no cost to you. Readers who have graduated from the same schools will have their interest pricked; and many will become fans, feeling a hometown link with a fellow alum when they read. And don't think you have to have multiple postgraduate degrees for this idea to work for you. Some of the best free promotion I have gotten came from my high school alumni paper."

School Visits

Bea Gormley is the author of the recently released historical novel, *Adara* (Eerdmans), set in ancient Israel and based on the story in 2 Kings 5. She has visited elementary and middle schools in California, Oregon, Florida, Massachusetts, and many states in between.

During her author visits, Bea tells how she became a writer. One of her goals in school visits is to sell books, but she also expands students' knowledge about book writing and publishing. She talks about reaching a goal through persistence. She explains that writing is hard and takes a lot of patience, but is rewarding. Bea has this suggestion for authors doing school visits:

When I first began to visit schools, one problem came up over and over: Children would ask me to sign a page in their notebooks or a loose piece of paper. I can't blame them for asking. Authors are presented to them as celebrities, and the one thing they know about celebrities is that fans ask for an autograph. I hated to say "no."

However, if you sign one child's piece of paper, you have to do the same for all the children—potentially hundreds at one school. I don't mind signing any number of my books, which at least have been paid for even if no one reads them.

But signed pieces of paper are just wastebasket fodder. And the signing takes up valuable time that I could better spend talking with the kids, reading aloud, or even finding the rest room.

My solution: When I'm invited to visit a school, I now offer to bring a signed bookmark for all the children I speak to, whether they buy one of my books or not. My bookmarks are easy to create in Word, four bookmarks to an 8-1/2" x 11" sheet of colored card stock. One side says, "Bea Gormley visits [name of school] on [date]," lists a few of my titles, and has my signature. The other side says, "Visit Bea Gormley online at www.beatricegormley.com." The school staff and parents always seem pleased to pass the bookmarks out to the kids, and the kids seem pleased to have them. And I'm pleased to have solved the autograph problem by promoting my books and my Web site!

Special Events

If you think you've seen Jan Coleman's name often in this book, you're right. Jan has such energy and so many creative ideas I had to include them all, including the Victorian tea that launched her book.

When ladies at her church asked what they could do to help celebrate the book, Jan suggested a Victorian tea. She offered to pay all the costs, and they didn't charge anything to come. Instead, they made it an outreach for their unchurched friends. "The church women brought their mix-and-match china teacups, platters, etc., decorated wonderful tables, and worked in the kitchen cutting up tea breads, etc. We had 140 women in dresses and hats who had a wonderful afternoon, and I spoke for forty minutes with a message from the book."

The excitement of the event itself would probably have been enough, but here's the good news. Jan sold nearly one hundred copies of her book, which, at her author discount, paid for the tea plus some. Since then, there's been a steady stream of buyers in the church bookstore, which can't keep the books in stock. (The store has ordered over one hundred books so far.)

Telephone Tag

Jan Coleman has written a book that ministers to hurting women, and she has contacted counseling centers in the greater Sacramento area where she lives. She gets many referrals from pastors in the area who are familiar with counselors who might be interested in a Christian book.

"The response has been wonderful. I've gotten letters and e-mails of recommendation from these counselors, which I use when contacting bookstores to keep them ordering the book, or to begin ordering it for potential customers."

Jan also has done well by contacting women's ministry directors at all the large churches in the area, sending them books, and following up with phone calls. She's sold books and gotten speaking invitations through her efforts. "This takes a bit of work, but it's well worth the effort. I started making the calls right before the book came out. Several of the women's ministry directors phoned me recently saying they just now got around to reading the book."

It takes time for momentum to get going, but phone calls and letters do pay off; and each sale can turn into a referral, especially with a book that reaches hurting people.

Textbook Sales

Carol Forseth released *Gentile Girl: Living with the Latter-day Saints* (Crossroads Press) in time to catch Olympic Fever in Salt Lake City. Once that marketing effort was over, she moved on to another creative way to sell books. "I've just finished a campaign targeting professors of comparative religions at Christian colleges, in hopes of them using the book as a textbook in their classes. I worked hard to come up with specific names of professors, using the Internet, and often calling the religion department to get the exact name. Then I sent a cover letter, a study guide for them to use with the book, some reviews, and an order form. They could get a copy by e-mailing me. Out of ten targeted schools, five professors requested review copies."

With persistence Carol could blanket schools with her book offering firsthand experience about Christianity and Mormonism.

Think Visual

Silvana Clark markets her own books and still has time to help her 12-year-old daughter, Sondra, with her books:

When sending out news releases, I always include a good, high-interest photo. It might be Sondra with paint on her face for her craft book, *Craft Fun with Sondra* (Meadowbrook

Press), or me peeking out from plants for my book *Parent-Tested Ways to Grow Your Child's Confidence* (Meadowbrook Press). Other times I wear a jungle outfit with pith helmet for my book *Taming the Marketing Jungle* (Hara Publishing).

I look for seasonal tie-ins. Sondra's craft book has lots of ways for me to send out articles or news releases on "Helping Kids Make Their Own Halloween Costumes" or "Easy Gifts Kids Can Make for the Holidays." For my parenting books, I write articles like "Help Your Child Start School with Self-Confidence" and "Summer Activities to Raise Your Child's Confidence."

When pitching TV producers, I never say, "Here's my book." Instead I say, "With summer approaching, parents are looking for ways to keep children busy. Would you be interested in a segment that offers fifteen ideas for low-cost summer fun?" Then, of course, the book gets mentioned. I always send thank-you notes and gifts to radio and television producers after I've been on the show."

Visual Aids

Diane Bisson is a self-published author of a series of self-help books for children, with versions for both Christian and secular markets. She says, "To promote them I have done presentations in schools, both public and private, as well as in Sunday schools. My presentations are complemented with doll-size puppets, where the children are invited to come up and role play the situations in the books. Following these presentations, I usually have a display table of my books where parents, teachers, and grandparents can come and purchase the books."

Volunteering

Judy Rushfeldt, author of *Freedom versus Feminism* (Life Tools Press), has found volunteering to be a way to build relationships with decision makers. She volunteers for a nonprofit family organization that sends out a fundraising letter every year. "I suggested they offer my book free for donations of $50 or more. I offered the book to them wholesale, so it wasn't a major expense to them. This was definitely a win-win situation, as the donations increased significantly and I sold about a thousand books through this fundraiser."

This is an idea that can work for many authors. Don't forget that nonprofit organizations have board members and others who get a gift each year for Christmas or other occasions. I sold a few hundred books to a charity I had written about in one of my books. Think about groups in your area and beyond who are a perfect match for your book and give them a call.

These are only a few ideas that you are welcome to place your own unique spin on to sell books. One wonderful thing about being an author in the family of God is that His children share. If you have ideas you'd like to share with other writers, please e-mail me at Carmen@writerspeaker.com. Every few weeks, I'll send the *You Can Marketing Ideas* newsletter to those who subscribe. I'd love to feature you and your idea. If you'd like to sign up to receive great marketing tips, visit www.writerspeaker.com/youcan.html and join the list.

Featured Authors

Neva Andrews	www.jobarkley.com
Wilburta Arrowood	www.wilburtaarrowood.com
Janet and Ron Benry	www.benrey.com
Diane Bisson	www.dilam.com
Janet and Stephen Bly	www.blybooks.com
Allison Bottke	www.godallowsuturns.com
Dianne E. Butts	www.dianneebutts.com
Silvana Clark	www.silvanaclark.com
Sondra Clark	www.sondrascrafts.com
Jan Coleman	www.jancoleman.com
Traci DePree	www.tracidepree.com
Rosey Dow	www.roseydow.com
T. Suzanne Eller	www.daretobelieve.org
Joan Esherick	www.joanesherick.com
Eva Marie Everson	www.evamarieeverson.com
Anne Fine	www.annefine.co.uk
Carol Forseth	www.gentilegirl.com
Beatrice Gormley	www.beatricegormley.com
Gail Hayes	www.daughtersoftheking.com
Randall Ingermanson	www.rsingermanson.com
Verla Kay	www.verlakay.com
Harry Kraus	www.cuttingedgefiction.com
Wendy Lawton	www.wendylawton.com

Caron Loveless   www.caronloveless.com
Marsha Marks   www.marshamarks.com
Janet Holm McHenry   www.janetmchenry.com
Brenda Nixon   www.parentpwr.com
Cherry Pedrick   http://marvelite.prohosting.
                           com/cherlene
Judy Rushfeldt   www.lifetoolsforwomen.com
Lauraine Snelling   www.laurainesnelling.net
Gary Stanley   www.garimus.com
Laura Jensen Walker   www.laurajensenwalker.com
Jim Watkins   www.jameswatkins.com

Featured Resources

Choice Books   www.choicebooks.org

Book Clubs

Authors on the Web   www.authorsontheweb.com
Good Girl Book Club   www.goodgirlbookclubonline.com
KidsRead.com   www.kidsreads.com
ReadingGroupGuides.com   www.readinggroupguides.com
TeenReads.com   www.teenreads.com

The Finished Product
Final Words

When I stand before God at the end of my life, I would hope that I would not have a single bit of talent left, and could say, "I used everything you gave me."

— Erma Bombeck

I t's all finished. I done builded you a chapel," Homer said to Mother Superior after he completed the finishing touches in *Lilies of the Field*. Homer surveyed his creation and smiled. Mother Superior, convinced things still needed to be done, questioned Homer about this and that, and his answer never varied, "Done."

Homer gathered the nuns for what would be their final English lesson. "I build a chapel," he said.

The smiling nuns repeated in lyrical, accented English, "I build a chapel."

Pointing a finger at the nuns, Homer moved on to the next pronoun. "You build a chapel."

Again the nuns parroted his phrase, "You build a chapel."

Homer had learned that building a chapel was a group effort and proudly proclaimed with a sweep of his hands, "We build a chapel."

"No," Mother Superior interrupted before the sisters piped in. Pointing toward heaven, she said, "He build a chapel."

And so it is with your book. It's easy to get caught up in the details and forget that back in chapter one you made God your contractor. It is from Him that all success flows.

As I began to write this book, I sent e-mails to members of several online Christian writers' groups. I asked published authors to share marketing tips that might be helpful to other authors. My friend, Martha M. Boshart, author of *Heaven: Who's Got the Tickets & How Much Do They Cost?* (Barbour), sent me her tip. In God's perfect timing, it arrived as I began writing the book's closing words. Her honest comments sum up the essence of this book and how we as Christian communicators should approach our marketing:

> In addition to the standard of bathing my book project in prayer, starting with long before it was a presentable manuscript and before I had a publisher, I have one simple marketing tool which is just right for this particular book. As you may know, I was soundly humbled when I found out Barbour was going to publish it as an inexpensive, mass-market paperback. I had the notion that the worth of a book and the credibility of its author were determined in large measure by its price.
>
> I do believe in the minds of many potential readers, there is a connection. But in my case, I think this was God's signal to me that this was not about the worth of my book, but the importance of its message. It was also not about me as its author, but about Jesus Christ, the Author of the message.
>
> Barbour's choice of medium has done two important things: First, it has made it affordable for me to make sure I always have books available to give at the prompting of the Holy Spirit. I get those promptings in some of the most unlikely places and at some of the most unpredictable times. I give a lot of books away. Secondly, it has made it very affordable for prospective readers to buy and often, in turn, to give away.
>
> Its humbling affordability has been transformed into my most valuable marketing tool, and I market without fanfare or ulterior personal agenda every single day. My last chapter is

about the Great Commission (Mark 16:15), and this is my tool
for carrying that out.

Jesus didn't have a fancy marketing plan. He didn't have a grand
media tour. There wasn't even any media in His day. In fact, not until
much later, Jesus didn't even have a book. God's message is all about
relationships: The relationship He has with His son. The relationship
His son has with us that He willingly died on the cross for our sins. The
relationship we have with the Holy Spirit once we have run into God's
open arms. The relationship we have with our Abba Father is such that
once we accept all that He so lovingly offers us, we are called to build
relationships with others to share the good news.

As you face discouragement in your marketing—and you will face
discouragement—you will most likely ask, "Why me?" It's natural to ask
that question when things aren't going your way. At that moment, please
remember why you wrote your book.

When your book is featured in *Christian Retailing,* when you are
asked to address thousands and you sell out of all the books you
shipped, be blessed. When you somehow do everything right and your
book goes into a second or third or tenth printing, give thanks. And
when someone sends you an e-mail, or tells you in person, that your
book is the reason she has accepted Jesus Christ as her personal Lord
and Savior, that is truly the time to ask, "Why Me?"

Mother Superior was right. Homer didn't build the chapel. God
built it through Homer and everyone who helped. You aren't the one
who will be able to take the credit if your book is a best-seller. God,
through your writing, is reaching people throughout the world.

I have written only one poem in my life, but I'd like to share it with
you at the end of this chapter. Your readers are asking, "Why me?" Your
words can help them be as thankful for the "Why Me?" times in their
lives as you are.

My prayer for you is that this book has in some way helped you to
understand how to get your book into the hands of those who need it as
they ask, "Why Me?"

Why Me?

by Carmen Leal

I gaze at the serene blue waters and wonder, "Why me?"
I ponder my shattered hopes and dreams and wonder, "Why me?"
I recall happier times and wonder, "Why me?"

Sitting on the barren beach with waves splashing against the shore,
I feel as empty as the horizon.
As a lone tear drips off my chin and splashes onto the rocks,
I believe I can fill the ocean with the tears I have shed.

When my turbulent emotions become placid,
I think of my beautiful sons and wonder, "Why me?"
I reflect on my health, my family, and friends
        and wonder, "Why me?"
I am blessed by thoughts of my church and wonder, "Why me?"

My mind fairly races with the joys of my life
I have somehow forgotten in my self-pity.

I consider a God so great He sent His son to die
        on the cross for me, and I wonder, "Why me?"
I am grateful that as Jesus hung on the cross
He didn't say, "Why me?"

Featured Author
Martha Boshart   www.marthaboshart.com

Recommended Books

Allen, Debbie. *Confessions of Shameless Self Promoters*, 2nd ed. Tempe, AZ: Success Showcase Publishing, 2002.

Bagnull, Marlene. *Write His Answer*, 2nd ed. Phoenix: Write Now Publications, 1999.

Bayan, Richard. *Words That Sell*. Chicago: Contemporary Books, 1987.

Haggerty, Deb (featured). The Sales Coach: Selling Tips from the Pros. Monroeville, PA: Imago Editions, 1997.

Herr, Ethel. *Introduction to Christian Writing*, 2nd ed. Phoenix: Write Now Publications, 1999. Horowitz, Shel. *Grassroots Marketing: Getting Noticed in a Noisy World*. White River Junction, Vt.: Chelsea Green Publishing Company, 2000.

Kremer, John. *1001 Ways to Market Your Books*, 5th ed. Fairfield, Iowa: Open Horizons, 2000.

Leal, Carmen. *WriterSpeaker.com: Internet Research and Marketing for Writers and Speakers*. Colorado Springs: WaterBrook, 2000.

Levinson, Jay Conrad, Rick Frishman, and Jill Lublin with Mark Steisal. *Guerrilla Publicity: Hundreds of Sure-Fire Tactics to Get Maximum Sales for Minimum Dollars*. Avon, Mass.: Adams Media Corporation, 2002.

Levinson, Jay Conrad, Rick Frishman, and Michael Larsen. *Guerrilla Marketing for Writers: 100 Weapons to Help You Sell Your Work*. Cincinnati, Ohio: Writer's Digest Books, 2000.

Littauer, Florence and Marita. *Talking So People Will Listen: You Can Communicate with Confidence*. Ann Arbor, Mich.: Servant Publications, 1998.

Mathis, Mark. *Feeding the Media Beast: An Easy Recipe for Great Publicity*. Purdue University, 2002.

Niederst, Jennifer. *Learning Web Design: A Beginner's Guide to HTML, Graphics, and Beyond*. Cambridge, Mass.: O'Reilly & Associates, 2001.

Osborn, Susan Titus. *Just Write!* Phoenix: Write Now Publications, 2000.

Osborn, Susan Titus, ed. *The Complete Guide to Christian Writing and Speaking*, 2nd ed. Phoenix: Write Now Publications, 2002.

Osborn, Susan Titus, ed. *Complete Guide to Writing for Publication*. Phoenix: Write Now Publications, 1999.

Poynter, Dan. *The Self-Publishing Manual: How to Write, Print and Sell Your Own Book,* 13th ed. Santa Barbara, Calif.: Para Publishing, 2001.

Ross, Marilyn and Tom. *Jump Start Your Book Sales: A Money-Making Guide for Authors, Independent Publishers and Small Presses.* Cincinnati, Ohio: Writer's Digest Books, 1999.

Stuart, Sally E. *Christian Writers' Market Guide.* Colorado Springs: WaterBrook, annual.

Order Form

#	Title	Price	Total
	A Complete Guide to Christian Writing and Speaking—Susan Osborn, Editor	$15.00	
	A Complete Guide to Writing for Publication—Susan Osborn	$15.00	
	An Introduction to Christian Writing—Ethel Herr	$17.00	
	How to Write and Sell a Christian Novel—Gilbert Morris	$12.00	
	Just Write—Susan Osborn	$12.00	
	Write His Answer—Marlene Bagnull	$14.00	
		SUB-TOTAL	
		+ S&H*	
		TOTAL	

*S&H: Add $4.00 shipping and handling for the first book and $1.00 for each additional book.

Purchase these books
from your local bookstore or contact:

Write Now Publications
5501 N. 7th Ave., #502
Phoenix, AZ 85013

800-931-BOOK (2665)